The Reminiscences of

Rear Admiral Kent C. Melhorn
Medical Corps, U.S. Navy (Retired)

and

Commander Charles M. Melhorn
U.S. Navy (Retired)

U.S. Naval Institute
Annapolis, Maryland
1983

Preface

This volume is a delight to read, as well as being a source of a good deal of solid historical information. It is also a rarity in that it contains two oral histories from the same family, a father and son, both of whom made careers of the Navy. Because of its considerable historical value and its wealth of entertaining stories, one's only regret is that the volume is not longer than it is.

The story begins shortly after the turn of the 20th century when Kent C. Melhorn was a young Navy doctor. His most vivid recollections from that period come from service in the Caribbean--operating off Nicaragua, serving with Colonel Joseph H. Pendleton and Medal of Honor winner Ernest Williams in Santo Domingo, and then two tours in Haiti. In the latter, during the mid-1920s, Dr. Melhorn had an enormous impact on public health in the country, demonstrating the value of modern medicine over voodoo practices. In the 1930s, Dr. Melhorn had an interesting assignment as attending physician to the World Disarmament Conference in Geneva, served at naval hospitals ashore, and was fleet surgeon on the staff of the Commander in Chief U.S. Fleet, J.M. Reeves. Melhorn later held the same billet under Admiral J.O. Richardson. During World War II, Admiral Melhorn served a valuable tour as commander of the Naval Medical Supply Depot in Brooklyn.

The second half of the volume comprises the recollections of Commander Charles M. Melhorn, an officer who has led a charmed life. During the Guadalcanal campaign in 1942, he survived the sinking of a PT boat and a case of pneumonia. Seeking aviation training as a means of escaping the rigors of the war zone, he wound up in a plane crash and was later in a midair collision after winning his wings. During the waning days of World War II, Melhorn earned the Navy Cross for torpedo plane strikes against the Japanese fleet. This memoir contains some particularly entertaining tales about Melhorn's service on the staff of the colorful Admiral "Jocko" Clark, and he later tells of a disastrous Sixth Fleet cruise in the USS Ticonderoga in the mid-1950s. Commander Melhorn ditched at sea at night in his Skyraider and later saved the ship from serious damage by having his men execute a "pinwheel" maneuver. After retirement, he became a history professor and wrote the Naval Institute Press book Two-Block Fox, which describes the rise of the aircraft carrier in the U.S. Navy. Despite his many brushes with death, Commander Melhorn has retained a delightful sense of humor.

Credit for evoking these fun-to-read memoirs goes to Commander Etta-Belle Kitchen, who conducted the interviews of both father and son. Ms. Susan Sweeney of the Naval Institute compiled the helpful detailed index for this volume.

Paul Stillwell
Director of Oral History
U.S. Naval Institute
September 1983

Rear Admiral Kent C. Melhorn, Medical Corps,
U. S. Navy (Retired)

Rear Admiral Melhorn was born in Kenton, Ohio, December 9, 1883. He attended the public schools in Kenton, had one year at University of Pennsylvania, Ada, Ohio, and graduated from the University of Pennsylvania Medical School in 1906. He was appointed Acting Assistant Surgeon with the rank of Lieutenant (junior grade) in August, 1907, and was advanced as follows: Assistant Surgeon with the rank of Lieutenant April 11, 1908; Lieutenant Commander, May, 1917; Surgeon with the rank of Commander, May, 1918; Medical Director with the rank of Captain, July 1, 1929; Rear Admiral, September, 1942.

Rear Admiral Melhorn's first assignment was to the Naval Hospital, Norfolk, Virginia (1907) from which he was posted to the Naval Medical School, Washington, D.C. for the standard orientation course for incoming medical officers. He then served in USS Wabash (1908), USS Yankee (1908), and on her sinking in Buzzards Bay, Massachusetts, to USS Dixie (1909). Shore duty at the Naval Hospital, Newport, Rhode Island, followed in 1911 after which came tours of sea duty in USS South Dakota (1913) and USS Denver (1914), the latter in Mexican and Nicaraguan waters. Transferred again to shore duty he began the first of several tours with the Marines: North Island (San Diego) (1914); the Marine Contingent at the Pan Pacific International Exposition (San Francisco) (1915); the Pan California International Exposition (San Diego) (1916); and as battalion surgeon with the 4th Marine Regiment in Santa Domingo (1916).

With the entry of the United States into World War I he returned again to the Naval Hospital, Portsmouth, Virginia, where he served as First Lieutenant, and during the catastrophic flu epidemic of 1917-1918 as head of the contagious fever wards. In 1920 he was ordered to Haiti, where he served with the occupation forces as Chief of the Haitian General Hospital, Port-au-Prince. This tour was interrupted by an extended convalescence at the Naval Hospital, Washington, D.C., following an airplane crash in Haiti. In 1923 he was ordered to a course of instruction in cardiology at Massachusetts General Hospital, Boston, Massachusetts, following which he returned to Washington, D.C. (1923) as Executive Officer of the Naval Medical School.

In 1927 he was posted to a second tour in Haiti, this time serving as a Treaty Official in the capacity of Director General of the National Public Health Service.

In 1930 he was ordered to the Bureau of Medicine & Surgery, Washington, D.C., where he served as Detail Officer. This tour was interrupted by several months' duty in 1932 as Physician to the U.S. Delegation to the Disarmament Conference, Geneva, Switzerland.

Dr. Melhorn returned to sea duty in 1933, serving as Senior Medical officer in the hospital ship, USS Relief, from which he was transferred in 1935 to the post of Fleet Surgeon under then-CINCUS, Admiral J.M. Reeves. In 1936 he came ashore as Executive Officer, Naval Hospital, San Diego, from which post he was transferred in 1938 to the Naval Dispensary, Long Beach, California, where he served as Medical Officer in Command. In 1939 he returned to sea as Force Surgeon, Battle Force under Admiral J.O. Richardson, and served as Fleet Surgeon, Battle Force once more when Admiral Richardson fleeted up to CINCUS in 1940.

Following Admiral Richardson's relief by Admiral H.E. Kimmel in January, 1941, Dr. Melhorn was ordered ashore to Command of the Naval Medical Supply Depot, Brooklyn, New York, a post which he held until his retirement in 1946 at age 62.

His active service completed, Admiral Melhorn settled into quiet retirement in Julian, California, a mountain hamlet east of San Diego, where he remained until Mrs. Melhorn's death two decades later. His final days were spent at the home of his son in Vista, California, where he died in 1978.

Admiral Melhorn's citations included a letter of commendation from SecNav Josephus Daniels for his "bravery, courage and devotion to duty" while serving as a member of the U.S. Expeditionary Forces in Santo Domingo in 1916, and the following medals and decorations:

- Mexican Service Medal
- Dominican Campaign Medal
- Marine Corps Expeditionary Medal
- World War I Victory Medal, West Indian Clasp & Bronze Star
- Haitian Campaign Medal
- Haitian Médaille Militaire
- Haitian Médaille d'Honneur et Mérite (1930 and 1936)
- American Defense (Fleet)
- World War II Theater Medal (American)
- World War II Victory Medal
- Legion of Merit
- Order of the British Empire, Grade of Commander

He held memberships in both the American College of Surgeons and the American College of Physicians.

Commander Charles M. Melhorn, U.S. Navy (Retired)

Commander Melhorn was born July 22, 1918, at the Naval Hospital, Portsmouth, Virginia. After attending primary and secondary schools in Washington, D.C., Haiti, and Southern California he graduated from the University of California, Los Angeles, in 1940.

He enlisted in the Navy as an apprentice seaman in September of that year. After a short cruise in the battleship USS New York, he was accepted as a reserve midshipman (V-7) and ordered to a course of instruction at the U.S. Naval Academy at conclusion of which he was commissioned Ensign in the Naval Reserve in May 1941.

His first commissioned service came as a student at the Armed Guard School (for merchantmen) at the Naval Academy, from which he was posted in July 1941, to the USS Gregory, a World War I destroyer converted to a fast destroyer/transport (APD). From Gregory he was transferred to her sister, USS Colhoun, in which he served until her sinking off Guadalcanal in 1942. Following his convalescence at a U.S. Navy Mobile Hospital in Auckland, New Zealand, he returned to Guadalcanal, being posted this time to Motor Torpedo Boat Squadron Three. Wounded in action in the sinking of PT-44, he was ordered back to the States, where he undertook flight training at the Naval Air Station, Grand Prairie, Texas, in the Spring of 1943.

He received his pilot's wings at the Naval Air Station, Pensacola, Florida, in September 1943, and was ordered to advanced training in torpedo planes (TBF) in Jacksonville, Florida. He completed advanced training at NAS Opa Locka (Miami) and was retained there as a flight instructor. In 1944 he was ordered to Torpedo Squadron 50, succeeding to command of the squadron on the death of the commanding officer in a plane crash. He took the squadron on board USS Cowpens, a CVL serving with the Fast Carrier Task Forces, and participated in the final Third Fleet strikes against Japan in 1945. During this series of engagements he was awarded the Navy Cross for leading the glide bombing attack that delivered the coup de grâce to the battleship Haruna at Kure, Honshu.

Following the war, Commander Melhorn received a regular commission and in 1946 was ordered to the newly-commissioned carrier, USS Leyte, in which he served as Flight Deck Officer. Following a tour at the Naval Air Station, Quonset Point, Rhode Island, he returned to sea as Flag Secretary, Commander Carrier Division Four under Admirals Jocko Clark, Matt Gardner and Cato Glover, who flew their flags in the carriers, USS Philippine Sea, Franklin D. Roosevelt, and Midway. Attendance at the General Line School, Monterey, California, followed in 1951, after which he served as Aviation Safety Officer on the staff of Admirals Albert Morehouse and Cato Glover, Chiefs of Naval Air Advanced Training at the Naval Air Station, Corpus Christi, Texas. In 1954 he was ordered again to NAS Quonset Point, Rhode Island, where he served as Operations Officer and later at Detachment Officer-in-Charge in Carrier Airborne Early Warning Squadron 12, the latter billet involving an extended cruise on board USS Ticonderoga with the Sixth Fleet.

In 1956 he was ordered as Executive Officer to the NROTC unit, Brown University, Providence, Rhode Island. Two years later he returned to sea as Air Operations Officer on the staff of Commander Carrier Division 15 under Admirals Red Sharp and Frank Brandley. In 1959 CarDiv 15 deployed in USS Kearsarge for an extended cruise with the Seventh Fleet. Returning to the States in 1960, Commander Melhorn was posted to the staff of General Laurence Kuter, USAF, CinC NORAD in Colorado Springs, Colorado, where he served until retired in 1961 by reason of physical disability.

Following retirement he received a Master's Degree at San Diego State University and in 1966 joined the History faculty there. At the same time he undertook doctoral studies at the University of California at San Diego, where he received his Ph.D. in 1973.

His doctoral dissertation was published by the Naval Institute Press the following year under the title Two-Block fox. At present (1983) he has a novel in progress and is active in civic affairs in the city of Los Angeles. He currently resides in Beverly Hills.

Commander Melhorn's academic career includes a BA from the University of California at Los Angeles, an MA from San Diego State University, an MA (ad eundam) from Brown University, and a Ph.D. from the University of California at San Diego.

He holds the following medals and decorations:

Navy Cross
Air Medal
Purple Heart
Presidential Unit Citation
Air Force Commendation
US Defense Medal (Atlantic Clasp)
World War II Asiatic-Pacific Theater Medal (4 battle stars)
World War II American Theater Medal
World War II Victory Medal
National Defense Medal

DECLARATION OF TRUST

The undersigned does hereby appoint and designate as his (her) Trustee herein, the Secretary-Treasurer and Publisher of the United States Naval Institute to perform and discharge the following duties, powers, and privileges in connection with the possession and use of a certain taped interview between the undersigned and the Oral History Department of the United States Naval Institute.

1. Classification of Transcript.

   (X)a. If classified OPEN, the transcript(s) may be read or the recording(s) audited by the qualified personnel upon presentation of proper credentials, as determined by the Secretary-Treasurer of the U. S. Naval Institute.

   ( )b. If classified PERMISSION REQUIRED TO CITE OR QUOTE, the user will be required to obtain permission in writing from the interviewee prior to quoting or citing from either the transcript(s) or the recording(s).

   ( )c. If classified PERMISSION REQUIRED, permission must be obtained in writing from the interviewee before the transcribed interview(s) can be examined or the tape recording(s) audited.

   ( )d. If classified CLOSED, the transcribed interview(s) and the tape recording(s) will be sealed until a time specified by the interviewee. This may be until the death of the interviewee or for any specified number of years.

2. It is expressly understood that in giving this authorization, I am in no way precluded from placing such restrictions as I may desire upon use of the interview at any time during my lifetime, nor does this authorization in any way affect my rights to the copyright of my literary expressions that may be contained in the interview.

Witness my hand and seal this 24th day of May 1970

[signature: Kent C. Melhorn]

I hereby accept and consent to the foregoing Declaration of Trust and the powers therein conferred upon me as Trustee:

[signature: Kent C. Melhorn]
[signature: R. E. Bowker Jr.]
Sec-Treas
US Naval Institute

DECLARATION OF TRUST

The undersigned does hereby appoint and designate as his (her) Trustee herein, the Secretary-Treasurer and Publisher of the United States Naval Institute to perform and discharge the following duties, powers, and privileges in connection with the possession and use of a certain taped interview between the undersigned and the Oral History Department of the United States Naval Institute.

(1) As an <u>Open</u> transcript. It may be read (or the tape audited) by qualified researchers upon presentation of proper credentials as determined by the Trustee.

(2) It is expressly understood that in giving this authorization, I am in no way precluded from placing such restrictions as I may desire upon use of the interview at any time during my lifetime, nor does this authorization in any way affect my rights to the copyright of any literary expressions that may be contained in the interview.

Witness my hand and seal this __16__ day of __September__ 19_70_

Charles M. Melhorn
Cdr USN (ret)

I hereby accept and consent to the foregoing Declaration of Trust and the powers therein conferred upon me as Trustee:

R. E. Bowker Jr.
Secretary-Treasurer and Publisher

Interview with Rear Admiral Kent C. Melhorn, Medical Corps,
         U.S. Navy (Retired)

Place: Admiral Melhorn's home in Julian, California

Date: 14 February 1970

Subject: Biography

Interviewers: Commander Etta-Belle Kitchen and
                Commander Charles Melhorn

Q: It's a real pleasure to be here, as you know. The Institute appreciates the time and thought I know you've given in preparing for this interview, Admiral, so first I'll ask you about when you were born and something about your early days.

Admiral Melhorn: I was born December 9, 1883, in the town of Kenton, Ohio. After graduation from high school and one year pre-medical work at Ohio Northern University in Ada, Ohio, I passed the examination for entrance to the medical school of the University of Pennsylvania in Philadelphia. After graduation there in the class of 1906 and one year's internship at the Lancaster General Hospital in Lancaster, Pennsylvania, I passed the examinations for entrance to the Naval Medical Corps as an acting assistant surgeon.

Q: What prompted you to be interested in the Navy?

Admiral Melhorn: Going back some years, my first longing

Kent Melhorn -

for a naval career occurred at the age of nine. I had been taken by my parents to visit friends in Portland, Oregon. It was there I was thrilled by the sight of the USS Charleston and Baltimore anchored in the Willamette River. They were there for the Rose Festival. Each night they flashed their searchlights over the city. I have never forgotten the thrill and ambition that seeing them inspired. My first assignment in the Navy was for a few weeks at the naval hospital in Norfolk, Virginia, followed by orders to attend the regular course for recently commissioned medical officers at the Naval Medical School in Washington.

Q: Is the grade, acting assistant surgeon, a grade that exists today?

Admiral Melhorn: No.

Q: Acting assistant surgeon, and you were a j.g.?

Admiral Melhorn: I took the examination in Philadelphia, because I didn't have enough money to go to Washington. If I had gone to Washington, I could have been commissioned an assistant surgeon.

Q: Why did you decide to go in the Medical Corps in the first place?

Admiral Melhorn: As I grew up, I had a great desire to go to the Naval Academy, and my father, who was active in political life in Ohio, was in a position to have gotten me an appointment to the Naval Academy, but after I found out that a young man who had been at the Naval Academy only one year had come home suddenly, we were very curious. In a short time I found out that he had bilged the Naval Academy in mathematics. When I heard that, I said to my father, "I never can go to the Naval Academy and get through." Mathematics was the bane of my existence and still is. So in talking to what later became my mother-in-law, I learned there were other ways to come into the service, and one of them was through the field of medicine. When I told my father I would like to study medicine, he breathed a sign of relief and took me to Philadelphia.

Q: I honestly would think medical school harder than the Academy. Your son Charley said it was the only time he had heard of a man getting into the Navy by going the hard route through medical school. I agree.

Admiral Melhorn: On graduation from the Naval Medical School in May 1908, I was assigned to the USS Wabash at the Boston Navy Yard. that ship had participated in the War Between the States and could no longer go to sea. My first morning aboard was one I'll never forget. I'd always heard that officers

Kent Melhorn -

coming out of the Naval Academy had had very strict training in the care of their room as well as sanitation in general, so before going to breakfast that morning in the wardroom, I spent over an hour cleaning up my room and getting it shipshape Having done that, and as I passed the room next to me--it was occupied by a recent graduate from the Naval Academy-- I never saw such a mess in my life. I thought I was getting off to a pretty good start. Arriving at the table, the president of the mess was a senior medical officer, and just as I sat down he came out with a roar, "Steward, there's a fly in here!" The steward came rushing in with a fly-swatter to get ahold of this fly. After meeting up with so many bugs, roaches, and so forth, in my years in the Navy, it is strange to remember that first experience with Navy sanitation.

My next assignment was to the USS <u>Yankee</u>, the Navy's first floating machine shop and mother ship for torpedo boats and submarines in the Atlantic. One day, out from New England coastal waters toward Newport, Rhode Island, in an intensely thick fog, the ship ran aground high up on what was called Hen and Chickens Reef in Buzzards Bay, not too far out from the town of New Bedford. The ship sustained about 12 holes in the hull and water poured in, engulfing everything below the wardroom deck, and we were hard, fast aground. There being danger that we might sink, the skipper ordered all hands to abandon ship. With a large seabag almost as tall as I was, I went from drawer to drawer in my cabin, dumping the contents of each drawer into the bag which was just inside the door. When the bag was filled, it was so heavy, and so blocked access to the wardroom, that I was no able to get out of my room. Whereupon I opened a large porthole in my room, and crawled up hand over hand to the upper deck in seconds flat. Two companies were employed without success to pull us off of the rocks, and it was not until a third company from New York with so-called "sand hogs" aboard--those were men who helped build the first tunnel under the Hudson River--the Merritt Scott Chapman Wrecking Company. So the entire top deck was sealed and air was pumped in from below. As the air came in, the water went out through the holes that had been sustained in the hull. A few days later, a tug maneuvering alongside trying to pull us off, banged in a porthole on one side of the ship, letting tons of water in, whereupon the ship sank. Some months later it was blown up in Buzzards Bay by the Army Engineers.

Q: It was a hazard to shipping, I presume. Was anyone on it when she went down?

Admiral Melhorn: No, we had all been taken off. This was my first and only experience in being shipwrecked. After two weeks, prior to the ship sinking, we were transferred to the Boston Navy Yard to await the findings of a board of investigation. Incidentally, the captain of that ship was a son-in-law of Admiral Bob Evans, who had taken the fleet around the world.* At the completion of the board of investigation procedure, we were ordered to the USS Dixie, a sister ship of the Yankee, and outfitted as a parent ship for torpedo boats and submarines.

After a cruise through the Caribbean, we returned to Hampton Roads where we picked up several hundred Marines from the battleships that had just returned from their cruise around the world. We took those Marines up to Washington to attend the inaugural parade for President Taft.**

Q: Did you see that parade?

Admiral Melhorn: Yes.

Q: Would you describe it?

Admiral Melhorn: I didn't have a grandstand seat; I had crawled up in a truck that had the back of it in such a position you could see the parade. I no sooner got up there and the cops came along and pulled that truck out of there, so I was left

---

*Rear Admiral Robley D. Evans, USN, was Commander in Chief U.S. Atlantic Fleet. His son-in-law, Commander Charles C. Marsh, USN, was commanding officer of the Yankee when she ran aground on 23 September 1908.
**President William Howard Taft was inaugurated in Washington on 4 March 1909.

standing alone on the side of the curb. I think the most interesting thing of that parade was to see the Philippine Constabulary Band shivering. It was very, very cold--snow had recently fallen--but they struggled along, and as they passed, they could hardly toot those horns.

In June 1911, I was ordered to duty at the Naval Hospital at Newport, Rhode Island, having at that time been promoted to the rank of passed assistant surgeon.

Q: What does passed assistant surgeon mean?

Admiral Melhorn: It means I passed the examination.

Q: They don't have that title today, do they?

Admiral Melhorn: No.

Nothing of any special interest occurred while I was at the naval hospital in Newport. In May 1913, I was ordered to the USS South Dakota at San Francisco. After being aboard there for about a month, I was suddenly detached to the USS Denver in June 1913, to take the place of a medical officer who had completed his duty afloat and was being ordered ashore. Nothing of any special interest occurred on the Denver. I recall one day being requested by some friends up in the town of Chinandega in Nicaragua, to bring a baseball team to have a game.

Kent Melhorn -

Q: What were you doing? Were you on a cruise?

Admiral Melhorn: We were anchored off Corinto, Nicaragua. It was just a regular patrol up and down the West Coast. We always kept a ship down there.

Q: You weren't there for any government intervention or anything like that?

Admiral Melhorn: No. While in Nicaragua I did make a trip up the railroad to Managua, where I had an old friend, Colonel Rixey, who was in command of our detachment up there.[*] He had been preceded by Smedley Butler. It was in Butler's time they had to quell a revolution up there. But while I was there, there wasn't anything going on. We went up to the town of Chinandega, laughing up our sleeve at being asked to go there and play a baseball game with the little team that they had, and lo and behold, they just licked the pants off us. They had probably the most famous pitcher that ever graduated from Cornell University whose name was John De Jean. He came from a French family that owned a big coffee ranch in Chinandega.

Q: And he was a native Nicaraguan?

---

[*]Presley M. Rixey, Jr., then Captain, USMC.

Admiral Melhorn: He wasn't a native. His family was from France and they had this big coffee "Finca," they called them, in Nicaragua.

In August 1914, I was ordered to the Fourth Regiment of Marines in North Island, San Diego, under the command of Colonel Joseph Pendleton, after whom Camp Pendleton is named. At that time the Army Air Corps had a small detachment there at what they called Rockwell Field. There were no Navy planes there at that time, but my little medical department was kept pretty busy seeing if we could be the first one to a damaged plane. We were having quite a number of crashes there, so it was always a race between my group and the little Army group as to who'd get there first.

Q: Was the North Island actually an island at that time? Was it, in fact, separated?

Admiral Melhorn: Yes. There was a little causeway that went over to Coronado. North Island at that time was just full of sagebrush and jackrabbits.

Q: Any installations there at all?

Admiral Melhorn: They had a little hangar there for the Army planes, but that was all.

Kent Melhorn - 1

Q: Where was the medical department stationed?

Admiral Melhorn: We were in tents.

Q: How long did that continue?

Admiral Melhorn: That must have continued until we broke up. On December 11, 1914, I accompanied a battalion of Marines to the Panama International Exposition in San Francisco. At the conclusion of that fair, we were ordered back to San Diego and went into camp where the naval hospital now is. We were in tents, at Balboa. After a few weeks there, we were suddenly ordered to entrain and were taken to New Orleans on our way to help quell a revolution in Santo Domingo. I recall marching down Canal Street, in New Orleans, on a terribly hot day. I was in a blue uniform--everyone else in khaki-- and it was quite an ordeal. We went aboard a ship called the Hancock, a transport, which landed us a few days later at a small port in Santo Domingo called Montecristi. There we went into camp preparing to march inland, which we did with Colonel Pendleton in command of the Marines. On the way up we had several small skirmishes with rebels.

Q: Why did the Marines go into Santo Domingo?

Admiral Melhorn: We landed there at the request of the Dominican

Government and our State Department to quell a revolution that was going on, and that was our mission. Spending a short time in the town of Santiago, I was ordered, with a battalion of Marines, further into the interior of a town called La Vega, which was the headquarters of this battalion. Early one morning, I received orders that there had been a battle by our forces in a town called San Pedro de Macoris, where we had a group of Marines under the command of a Lieutenant Bill Williams.* Williams was quite a character. He had been a member of a famous football team at Quantico and was, I think, the finest soldier man that I ever experienced in my 40 years in the Navy. Absolutely fearless, terrible alcoholic, but a splendid leader of men. He started his morning with a full glass of rum before breakfast. I used to plead with him that he was going to go to the dogs if he kept that up, but nothing would stop him. Anyway, he decided that he would capture the fort there manned by Dominicans. So at taps one evening, as the colors were being lowered, he led a group of 12 Marines up to the entrance to the fort. They saw him coming and tried to slam the door but with his big football feet he blocked that. They shot the light out over the gate, and from then on it was shooting at flashes. He captured the fort, but he had eight of his men quite badly wounded and that was the reason I was sent for. I was able to take

---

*First Lieutenant Ernest C. Williams, USMC, who won the Medal of Honor for his actions in Santo Domingo.

Kent Melhorn - 1

care of them all right, and they sent a hospital ship some days later.

Q: Were you the only doctor with the group?

Admiral Melhorn: Yes. I had some corpsmen.

Q: You must have been awfully busy.

Admiral Melhorn: We were.

Q: Were you a battalion surgeon or were you a regimental surgeon?

Admiral Melhorn: Battalion.

Having mentioned Bill Williams, I might add this. Some years later, I happened to be a patient in the naval hospital in Washington, and in the next room from me was a very prominent newspaperman, as well as a writer, Laurence Stallings was his name, who wrote the play What Price Glory?, which became a tremendous success. So on visiting back and forth in his room from time to time, he told me that the Sergeant Quirk in What Price Glory? was built around my old friend Bill Williams Sometime later, while I was still in the hospital, Bill Williams, who had gone through the war in France, was brought in as a patient, and I met up with him again.

I said, "Bill, what are you going to do?"

He said, "If I can't get my old friend to get me another assignment, I'll retire and go home and probably peddle newspapers on the street in my home town."

I said, "Who is this old friend?"

He said, "He's been helping me for years. Every time I'd want to get another assignment, I'd write him a letter and say that I wanted this or that duty."

I said, "Bill, who is this?"

He said, "Oh, he's known everywhere. Uncle Joe Cannon." He was a great power in Congress in his day.*

In the meantime, the war was coming on, and I was anxious to get back to the States and because I'd had, with one exception, more duty with Marines than any other doctor in the Navy, I thought I would be transferred to Quantico and go with one of the regiments to France.

Q: How long were you in Santo Domingo?

Admiral Melhorn: About 13 months.

Q: While you were still in Santo Domingo, did you have any personal acquaintance with Colonel Pendleton?

---

*Joseph G. Cannon served in the House of Representatives for nearly 50 years, holding the post as Speaker of the House from 1903 to 1911.

Kent Melhorn - 1

Admiral Melhorn: Oh yes. After landing at Montecristi, we had a two-hour battle on the way up at a place called Guayacanas. It was pretty hot there for a while; the shells were flying right and left, and I was rather busy doing what I could with some of the wounded. As I was going up to the front, scared stiff--I had never been in a real battle before--I happened to turn to my right and there I saw Colonel Pendleton sitting in an old Ford car, reading the Saturday Evening Post. Well, I thought, if he isn't worried, why should I be? I've never forgotten that, going into battle reading the Saturday Evening Post.

Q: Was he highly regarded by his troops?

Admiral Melhorn: Oh yes. He was very well liked.

Q: I don't want to leave Santo Domingo without mentioning that you received a letter of commendation from Josephus Daniels, who was then the Secretary of the Navy. Let me just point out that you were "brave, courageous, and devoted." I'm sure those things are true.

Admiral Melhorn: So instead of going to France, I was ordered to the naval hospital in Norfolk, Virginia, and as I've often thought that over, why didn't I get to France with all that duty I'd had with the Marines? I feel that because I had German in my name--Melhorn is a German name--and people with German names in World War I were having a little difficulty getting to France. Well, the duty at the naval hospital in Norfolk was a pretty strenuous one. I was placed in charge of the contagious disease camp, which was in tents, and it was a terrible winter. We had no heat except oil stoves. In making my rounds one day, I found one of my corpsmen had gotten ahold of some bricks, and he'd take a brick and wrap it in a flannel cloth, put it on top of the stove until it got good and warm, then he'd sell that to a patient for twenty-five cents. There was even some gouging going on in those days.

Q: I would have thought people would have died for lack of proper heat.

Admiral Melhorn: There was a great plea, of course, from the commanding officer to do something about this situation down there. We were having a terrible epidemic of cerebral spinal fever, called in those days meningitis, and also measles, and pneumonia. So the government finally erected semipermanent buildings, wooden buildings with wooden floors and they put big steam lines in, so it really made it quite comfortable.

Q: How many people would you have had in those tents?

Admiral Melhorn: Oh, the tents we had, you might squeeze in 12 in a tent. And there were hundreds of tents.

Q: Would you say that one of the reasons for the severity of the later influenza epidemic was that there had been a general weakening of resistance of the population due to the previous epidemics of meningitis and measles, and so forth?

Admiral Melhorn: No. This was coming all over the country. So much so that my commanding officer, Captain Spratling, received a telephone call one day from the commandant of the navy yard at Norfolk, who was very much concerned, because everyone knew that the flu was coming.* He said to Captain Spratling, "What is the most important thing we can do to be prepared for this epidemic?"

And Captain Spratling's reply was, "Build coffins." And that is exactly what happened. The commandant turned everybody over who could wield a hammer and drive a nail, and they built hundreds and hundreds of coffins, and we needed them badly up where we were because our morgue was chock full of bodies. They were dying like flies, and they couldn't be buried, so we just stored these bodies in the morgue until they could build enough coffins. That's how bad it was.

---

*Captain Leckinski W. Spratling, MC, USN.

Kent Melhorn - 17

Q: I imagine you were practically exhausted, yourself. Tell me about the hours and your work.

Admiral Melhorn: We worked day and night. Before I was detached from the camp and ordered up into the big hospital where I assumed the duty of first lieutenant--I think I was the first lieutenant in the medical corps at that time. The first lieutenant was sort of an assistant executive officer. I made the rounds, did the inspecting, and helped with the upkeep and repair. But before I was ordered up to the hospital, the exec called me one day, and he said, "I've got a problem."

I said, "What's the trouble?"

He said, "There's a yeomanette coming in with the mumps, and we don't have any place up here to take care of her. Can you help out?"

Well, I always made it a point to say, "Aye, aye, Sir."

How to do it, I didn't know, but when she came into the hospital she was transported down to my camp. In the meantime, I'd cleared out a brig and fixed it up. We had Navy nurses there to help us, so we made a pretty nice room for her. A couple of weeks went by, and she got along fine. One day one of my doctors--I had four doctors down there--came to me and he said, "We're going to have to change the diagnosis."

I said, "What's the trouble? Any complications?"

And he said, "Yes, she's pregnant." Well, in those days,

whenever you made a diagnosis, you always had to put under origin, was it, or was it not in the line of duty? That was a question for us. Being good old Marines and Navy men we decided "line of duty," and that's what she was given. For the good of the cause.

Q: You went through the war there at Norfolk with all of the rationing and everything that that entailed. Weren't you kind of running your own commissary there? You were occupying government quarters at the naval hospital; what did you have in the back yard?

Admiral Melhorn: Oh, we had a great big garden, and we also bought a cow. Charlie was born at that time and we needed plenty of milk, so I bought a cow.* This was a wonderful cow--she gave quarts and quarts of milk every day, so we spread the word around that we had this excess milk and we gave it to everybody who needed milk for their children. They were mostly families on the station.

Commander Melhorn: I think it's interesting that people think of officers' quarters nowadays as pretty starchy environment, yet not too many years ago there were cows in the back yard.

Q: That was a real rugged three years, though. The experience

---

*Charles M. Melhorn, who helped conduct this interview, was born 22 July 1918.

that you had and the time of the world then were just teeming
with incidents that should be told.

Admiral Melhorn: Well, when I mentioned these bodies that
we stacked in the morgue, it was a room about this size, about
20 feet by 14 feet, about 8 feet high and all the way to the
ceiling. It was awful.

Q: How long did you keep them there?

Admiral Melhorn: Sometimes as much as two weeks.

Q: Was there any refrigeration?

Admiral Melhorn: No. Formaldehyde.

Q: How many people died, did you know?

Admiral Melhorn: Hundreds.
   In 1920 I was ordered to Haiti, in charge of the Haitian
General Hospital. This was under the Haitian-American Treaty.

Q: Were there any particulars on that set of orders? Any
particular reason why you would be ordered to Haiti?

Admiral Melhorn: No, unless it was some success I had had

in that contagious disease camp.

Q: But you had no specialty in tropical medicine?

Admiral Melhorn: Well, I had been graduated from the Naval Medical School, and that was one of the main courses we had.

Q: Then all graduates of the Naval Medical School received a special course in tropical medicine?

Admiral Melhorn: That's right.

Q: Is this the course you took in Washington?

Admiral Melhorn: Yes.

Q: Well, I would imagine that the experience that you had in Norfolk would have been remarkably good experience for Haiti.

Admiral Melhorn: It must have been something in my record that they picked me out to go down to Haiti, and the fact that I'd also been in Santo Domingo.

Q: What was your grade then, Admiral?

Admiral Melhorn: Still passed assistant surgeon. That corresponds to a lieutenant. So in 1920, ordered to Haiti in charge of the Haitian General Hospital in Port-au-Prince.

Q: Was that the number two billet down there? You had one officer in the Medical Corps senior to you?

Admiral Melhorn: Yes, Commander McLean.*

Q: Why was an American medical officer ordered to a Haitian hospital?

Admiral Melhorn: Well, the Haitians had practically no doctors. They had a few who had been educated in France, but they weren't much good. At any rate, that's all we had to work with, so I had Navy nurses there with me. Later they were replaced by American Red Cross nurses. And of course, the Catholic Sisters had been in Haiti almost since the days of the French Revolution. The Catholic Sisters were really what stood between utter savagery and civilization. They did a heroic piece of work there. They were nursing sisters. The mother superior was probably the most beautiful woman that I have ever met. She had been born in Brittany, France, and took orders and was transferred to Canada, in a mother house up there, where she learned to speak English, and she spoke it beautifully.

---

*Commander Norman T. McLean, MC, USN.

She had a group of 12 nuns there in the compound for the hospital and did a marvelous piece of work.

Q: Did the Haitian Government ask for you? Did they ask for medical assistance from the United States?

Admiral Melhorn: Yes, under the treaty. The reason that the American forces were in Haiti occurred in 1915 (that was before I got there), when the German Government was about to seize Haiti. To prevent that, our government sent a cruiser under the command of Captain Caperton.* He landed some Marines at the dock there, and as they were marching into the city of Port-au-Prince, down from the head of the dock came a German attaché, I guess it was, with a few others and they were about to tell our people to get out of there, that the Germans were going to take over. I don't know what the reply was, but it was similar to what was made in World War II--"Nuts to you." And they disappeared. That's how we happened to get into Haiti in 1915.

Commander Melhorn: But the real reason was to preserve order because of the murder of President Sam; so this was the excuse that the Germans and the United States seized on to make an opening in the country.**

---

*Rear Admiral William B. Caperton, USN, Commander Cruiser Squadron Atlantic Fleet, arrived in Haiti 23 January 1915 in the armored cruiser Washington.
**The U.S. Marines landed on 28 July 1915 at Bizoton, three miles from Port-au-Prince, in the wake of the murder of Haiti's President Vilbrun Gjuillaume Sam.

Admiral Melhorn: That's right. President Sam had ordered the assassination of hundreds of prisoners they had locked up in a prison there, whereupon the populace arose and they grabbed him and cut his head off. They put his head on a spike and they marched all around the city with it. Incidentally, that old desk in the corner of this room was originally purchased by President Sam in Paris and brought to Port-au-Prince. It was years later that it was available for sale in the home that had been President Sam's.

Q: What was the German reason for interest in Haiti?

Admiral Melhorn: They wanted to get an approach to the Panama Canal. Of course, our government didn't want that to happen, so we took over Haiti. And of course, the same thing would have applied in Santo Domingo.

Q: Did the Germans have any warships there then?

Admiral Melhorn: Not then, but they were about to have some. We took it in order to protect the approaches to the Panama Canal, because if the Germans had had that, they would have complete control of the waterways leading toward the canal.

Q: But the Haitians had their own government. We simply

went in at their request to take care of the hospital?

Admiral Melhorn: That's right.

Q: And did we have military forces there, too?

Admiral Melhorn: Yes, we landed Marines in abundance.

Q: It was not only the hospitals, it was all facets of the Haitian Government that we controlled.

Admiral Melhorn: Oh yes. We had a financial advisor from the State Department who took over the finances; we had a representative from the Department of Agriculture--he brought a great big crew down there and created a school for agronomy. The Marines were in great abundance. They established a Haitian Army--they called it "Garde d'Haiti." There were civil engineers naval officers--Ben Moreell was head of the civil engineers.[*] He later became Admiral Moreell--Chief of Bureau of Yards and Docks.

Q: So the medical part of the Navy was simply part of the whole picture of American endeavor. Do you have a description of the hospital?

---

[*]Lieutenant Ben Moreell, CEC, USN, assistant engineer, Haiti.

Admiral Melhorn: This hospital could take care of about 200 patients, I would say. One long building and several smaller ones; they were just one-story affairs. Some of them had been built in the days of the French occupation, in Napoleonic times, and very badly run down until we took over. The common diseases were malaria, yaws, intestinal parasites, tuberculosis, vitamin deficiencies, dengue, dysentery, and tetanus.

Q: Why that, I wonder?

Admiral Melhorn: Well, the births occurred out in the brush largely around Haiti, and these old midwives would take mud, after they cut the cord, and plaster that, and of course, it was full of tetanus germs. We had an awful lot of that. We also had some rabies. I recall one day seeing a young man brought into the main gate, and he had a belt around him, and from this belt ran four ropes. At the end of each rope was a man bringing him in. He had hydrophobia and they were afraid of him, so each man was on a rope. Of course, he died.

Then we had a very severe epidemic of smallpox, which had come over on a fishing boat from Jamaica. We knew there was smallpox in Jamaica, but the British Government wouldn't call it smallpox; they called it Alastrim. The reason they didn't call it smallpox was that they didn't want anything to interfere with the tourist trade. Anyway, this thing swept through Haiti, totally unvaccinated, millions of people, and until we could get them vaccinated, they were dying like flies. Here were our Marines, thousands of them, and here were the Haitians dying like flies, and not a single case among our Marines. It was the greatest illustration of the effectiveness of vaccine ever on record, I believe.

Q: Did the Haitians have any resistance to being vaccinated?

Admiral Melhorn: At first they didn't want it done at all. They had their own voodoo method of treating things. Finally we obtained the help of the sisters and especially the priests, so every Sunday morning, at the conclusion of a service of their churches, all over the island, we would have our representative at the entrance of the church, on the steps outside and as they came out we vaccinated them. We eventually stopped the epidemic.

While on duty in Port-au-Prince at the Haitian General Hospital, I received a telephone call one day from a fellow medical officer on the south coast of Haiti, a town called Jacmel, that one of his children was seriously ill and he asked for help; so I volunteered to go. It would mean an eight-hour ride on horseback or a half an hour ride in a plane. So I asked for a plane from the Marines, and they gave it to me. All their regular pilots were off on duty somewhere, so they gave me a sergeant in the Marines, who was experienced, but not quite as well as a number one pilot. We flew over the mountains, about 6,000 feet maybe.

Q: What were you in?

Admiral Melhorn: We called them the Jenny, another name was "flyin coffin." There was no air field in Jacmel but a fairly good beach. So we landed on the beach, but we wound up on the nose of the plane. We'd hit a big cactus bush on the beach. Nobody was hurt; the pilot got out and he said he thought it was all right. I went about my business up the hill and did what I could to take care of the child, and when I came back, he assured me that everything was all right, so we took off. We got up practically over Port-au-Prince, about 6,000-7,000 feet, and I heard this thing, "pop--pop", and I knew we were in trouble of some kind. The last I remember, I remember bracing myself, because we were headed down like we were going into a spin, and we landed in the mangrove bushes on the beach at Port-au-Prince. I was completely knocked out. I had a concussion. I awakened and I heard some chopping sound, and I tried to get up out of this seat I was in, and found I couldn't. I noticed something had happened to my left leg, and it turned out I had a compound fracture of both bones of my left leg and of my nose. The noise that I heard

Kent Melhorn - 2

were the Marines with their machetes chopping their way in to get us. I was asked if I wanted to go to the Marine hospital or my own, and I said to take me to my own. I was there for a couple of months.

Commander Melhorn: Didn't you have some problems on the operating table with the anesthesiologist?

Admiral Melhorn: They had to give me a general anesthetic to take care of me. They called a medical officer from the Marine hospital to give me the anesthetic, and when he arrived, I saw what shape he was in--he was drunk. I just waved him away; I wouldn't let him touch me. So I called for my own anesthetist--in those days I was doing a little surgery myself. He was a black man, a Haitian, and a darned good anesthetist, too, so he took over. They put me to sleep and put a cast on, but they didn't put it long enough; they only put it up to my knee and it should have been up to my hip joint, so after about two months, when they took the cast off, I had non-union, it was just like a piece of rubber. I had visions of being sent back to the States and getting a bone graft--sliding graft they called them in those days. Well, they sent a hospital ship in from Guantanamo, the old Solace, and took me to Washington and put me in the naval hospital. The surgeon that came to take care of me gave me a very good examination and said,

Kent Melhorn - 29

"Melhorn, you don't need any operation. My surgery is going to be beefsteak and onions." That's what it was. I was lacking in vitamins, and that's the way they took care of me.

Q: And, of course, it knit perfectly, because you're in perfect shape now.

Admiral Melhorn: Oh, yes.

Q: Was that your first airplane ride?

Admiral Melhorn: Yes, it was the first one, and I've been scared to ride in one ever since.

Q: That was how you got out of Haiti after your first tour then. You didn't go back at this time?

Admiral Melhorn: After I had recovered at the naval hospital in Washington, I returned to Haiti and completed my tour. Then in 1923, I was ordered to Boston to take a special course in internal medicine at the medical school at Harvard, but more particularly, of the Massachusetts General Hospital in Boston, where I had the great opportunity to sit under the tutelage of the most famous cardiologist this country has ever produced, Dr. Paul White. It was a very interesting and splendid course for any doctor, and I was particularly impressed because I hadn't requested that course. I was delighted to have it and was most appreciative.

Within about two weeks before the course was completed, I got into a very embarrassing position. I had received a postcard from my mother-in-law, back in Ohio, stating that she had met an old classmate on the train coming back from Columbus, Ohio, up to her home, and it turned out to be Senator Fess.* Senator Fess occupied a tremendous political position in Washington. They called him Mr. Republican, and he was a great power in Congress. She asked Senator Fess, would he use his best influence to have me ordered to the naval hospital in San Diego? Here I hadn't asked for this course, and if Senator Fess would go up to the Surgeon General's office and ask that I be assigned to San Diego, what in the world would he think of me? I thought it over that night and decided in the morning to write him a personal letter. I was not a personal friend of the Surgeon General, who was Admiral Stitt,** but I wrote him that I had received this notice from my mother-in-law who was meddling in my affairs, and that if Senator Fess or any of his representatives should come to his office and ask that I be ordered to San Diego, or anywhere please consider that I am not behind that. I had nothing

---

*Senator Simeon D. Fess.

**Rear Admiral Edward R. Stitt, MC, USN, Surgeon General, U.S. Navy and Chief of the Bureau of Medicine and Surgery.

at all to do with it and in proof of that I enclosed the postcard which I had received from my mother-in-law. I never had a reply from the Surgeon General, but within a week I was ordered to the Naval Medical School to take the chair of medicine. I thought that was rather strange, but, of course, I was highly pleased. How in the world would that thing happen, and I decided that when the Surgeon General learned that Senator Fess was a very close friend of members of my family, it might not be a bad idea to have me ordered to Washington. Maybe I would be able to help get some of the appropriation bills through. Well, whether there's any truth to that or not, I don't know, but that's the way I rationalized it. So I was ordered to the Naval Medical School to help teach the younger doctors and so forth.

Q: How many doctors were in the Navy then?

Admiral Melhorn: There must have been at least 200.

Q: Do you remember how many there were when you went in the Navy?

Admiral Melhorn: When I went in, there were 53 vacancies. I don't recall how many were in the corps. One day while I was sitting in my office there at the Naval Medical School,

I was going over some papers and I sensed that there was someone in the door to my office. I just wanted to finish a last sentence, so I didn't look up right away, and when I did who should be standing in the door of my office but Mrs. Coolidge.* I jumped to my feet and apologized. She started to laugh and told me to sit down, that she was just out for a walk. She had walked from the White House up to the Naval Medical School which must have been at least a mile. She had been followed by a Secret Service man, of course, but she came into my office alone. She had come to see a member of the Cabinet, the Secretary of Agriculture, who was sick and in SOQ. So I called a nurse immediately and she took her over. Mrs. Coolidge was a wonderful woman--100% in every way that you wanted to think of her. After she had finished her visit in the sick officers' quarter, she came and stopped by the office to thank me again, and the nurse, for giving her some help. In the meantime, it had begun to rain, and the White House sent a car for her. The car was parked, and people were all lined up to see her get into the car. The car started down toward the main gate, and got about halfway down, when I noticed the car backing up to the entrance again. So I dashed to the door with an umbrella. Mrs. Coolidge got out of the car under my umbrella and came in. She said, "Doctor, I just forgot to say good-bye to the nurse." That's how thoughtful she was. It made quite an impression with me.

---

*Grace Anna Goodhue Coolidge, who was First Lady from 1923 to 1929.

Well, in the latter days of the Naval Medical School, my phone rang one day and it was the detail officer in the Bureau of Medicine and Surgery, Dr. Smith,* calling me, and he said, "Melhorn, your name is coming up under the wire and we'd like to know where you'd like to go on your next assignment?"

I said, "Thanks for the consideration. I'd like to go to the transport Henderson."

He said, "Why do you want to go there?"

I said, "Well, it has a very nice medical department, it has Navy nurses aboard, a fine group of corpsmen, and they carry men, women and children, and I want to keep my hand in clinical medicine--bedside medicine."

He said he would talk to the Surgeon General about it and call me back. The next morning he called and said, "Melhorn, you can't go to the Henderson."

I said, "I'm awfully sorry. Can you tell me where I'm going?"

He said, "You're going to Haiti."

I said, "I've had one tour of duty on Santo Domingo, and I've had one tour in Port-au-Prince, Haiti; now do I have to go back again?"

He started to laugh and he said, "Yes, but before you go back, you've got to go to New York. The Surgeon General wants you to go up to New York, and there's been an engagement

---

*Captain George T. Smith, MC, USN.

made for you with Dr. Vincent, who's the head of the Rockefeller Foundation.* The foundation wants to be of considerable assistance in the field of medicine, sanitation, and nursing in Haiti, and they're going to spend millions down there. The Surgeon General wants you to go back, if the foundation puts their 'OK' on you, because they want to establish a medical school, a training school for native nurses, so you are to go back and be in complete charge of all of it." All of this under the treaty, of course. So I had a delightful conversation with Dr. Vincent and apparently passed the grade all right, because shortly I received orders to return to Haiti to become the chief of the public health service down there. They called it "Service de général", and it turned out to be one of the high points of my career. We were operating 12 hospitals, 123 rural clinics, and a few traveling clinics back in the mountains. If I do say so, we did a marvelous job. It attracted a great deal of attention in the Navy and even in the States. The New York Times sent one of their top men down, Clarence Streit, who was one of their great writers, and he made a personal survey; I had a long interview with him, and when he went back to New York, he wrote a beautiful article about the work we were doing.**

---

*Dr. George E. Vincent.
**Clarence K. Streit, "Fourth of Haitians Patients at Clinics," the New York Times, 25 March 1928, Section 3, pages 1 and 8. One of the subheads over the article reads: "Dr. Melhorn, Sanitary Chief, Has Faith in Natives and Promotes Them in Medical Service."

Q: What was the nature of the rural clinics?

Admiral Melhorn: They were small buildings that we put up, and manned them--more or less first aid, you might call it.

Q: But they weren't permanently manned, were they?

Admiral Melhorn: Semipermanent. If we had anybody that had any sense of medicine at all, we would employ them, but we also used hospital corpsmen from the Navy. Generally, they were chief pharmacists, or pharmacist's mates, and they would live out in these rural places.

Q: That was an odd assignment, I'm sure, for a Navy man, wasn't it?

Admiral Melhorn: Oh yes. They learned to speak the patois, you know.

Q: You would have a chief hospital corpsman then, who would be, in effect, a practicing doctor of medicine out there.

Admiral Melhorn: That's right. Until we could get some Haitians trained.

Kent Melhorn - 3

Q: As far as the Haitians knew, this enlisted man was actually the doctor?

Admiral Melhorn: That's right, and they welcomed him, too.

Q: How many people were you responsible for--your entire staff, do you recall?

Admiral Melhorn: Well, I had six doctors with me at the Haitian General Hospital--they were members of my own corps. For instance, Lucius Johnson, I had him brought down, and he was in charge of the Haitian General Hospital.* I had several pharmacists. At each of these 12 hospitals that I mentioned, there was a naval medical officer. I had picked them and had them brought down from the States.

Q: How were they staffed? One of your doctors?

Admiral Melhorn: They'd have a pharmacist, chief pharmacist's mate, and the sisters, of course, were doing the actual nursing in these outlying hospitals. We didn't have enough Navy nurses to spread around for that.

Q: Was it your philosophy that as soon as a Haitian, a black man would become qualified, he would take over the functions

---

*Commander Lucius W. Johnson, MC, USN.

in one of these rural clinics and at that point you would bring your man back in, so that what you were trying to do was work all of yourselves out of a job?

Admiral Melhorn: That's right.

Q: And you said that one of your jobs was to train nurses.

Admiral Melhorn: That's right. And with the help of the sisters, we were able to select quite a nice group of Haitian girls, and they went into training with our Navy nurses helping, and the sisters. They did a fine job. As you mentioned, as the Haitian doctors became enough skilled to take over one of these hospital clinics, why, that was part of the performance, and he did.

Commander Melhorn: I think that's very interesting, because the United States has been accused, and is being accused, many times because of its so-called imperialistic practices, and you can hardly call this imperialism, within the accepted connotation now, whereby you were simply trying to work yourself out of a job.

Admiral Melhorn: The service that I was in, the public health service, did so well that we were directed by the President to be the first group pulled out of Haiti, and they sent us word through the State Department that we were to leave. And that was about two months before I actually did leave. So I pulled a Haitian doctor in, from the town of Jeremie, who was a black man, black as ink, but had done a magnificent job for us down there, and I wanted that recognized, and I also wanted to promote him. So I brought him into Port-au-Prince to take over my job in the main office.

Q: What had his education been?

Admiral Melhorn: He had been a member of the group selected to be sent to Europe for medical work. After arriving in Port-au-Prince on my second tour, I, with the help of a couple of Haitian doctors that I had become acquainted with on my first tour, selected a group of aspiring young men in Haiti who wanted to become doctors for fellowships, and we sent (under the Rockefeller Foundation paying all this bill) them to Germany, France, England, and the United States. These doctors went to these various countries and spent a year, year and a half, some of them two years; then they came back and became members of the faculty at the medical school that we had established in Port-au-Prince.

Q: Was that all the medical training they had had, those two and a half years?

Kent Melhorn - 39

Admiral Melhorn: Yes, if we'd stayed longer, they might have had more, but that helped a lot. I remember one of them came back from Germany with a white wife--that leads me up to the color line. After I had pulled in this doctor from Jeremie to take over my job, two days later I was waited upon by a group from the medical school, Haitian doctors. They came in to see me, and I was curious what it was all about. They came to protest my appointment of this doctor I had brought in to take my place. I said, "This man has a marvelous record, he deserves a promotion, and I'm sure he will be a good credit."

They said, "You can't do that; he's a black man." Now these men who had been waiting for me were mulattoes. They have a color line among themselves. I paid no attention to that; I made it stick. But within a month after I left, he was fired.

Q: Where did you live when you were in Haiti the second time?

Admiral Melhorn: Same place I lived the first time I was there. We had a very nice home up on the hill that was owned by a Haitian doctor.

Q: For some reason or other, I was picturing that the first time you lived in connection with the hospital.

Admiral Melhorn: No, we had a very nice home, up the hill,

which we enjoyed.

Q: What was your transportation?

Admiral Melhorn: Motor car.

Commander Melhorn: We had four horses. We had a stable in the back yard, and everyone had a riding horse.

Admiral Melhorn: One of the interesting experiences that Mrs. Melhorn had there--Mrs. Melhorn was a very good pianist and we had a nice piano in the home there--she became acquainted with an elderly Haitian who had been a member of the senate in Haiti. As a young man he had been educated in Leipzig, Germany, as a mining engineer. At the same time, he learned and loved music, and he played beautifully. Mrs. Melhorn struck up quite an acquaintance, and every Sunday morning he would walk down the hill to our place, and they would sit at the piano and have themselves a musical morning. From him, I heard this interesting story--when he was just a young shaver, his father became the first minister from Haiti to the United States. What I'm telling you is confirmed by one of the volumes that I have here of Harper's Weekly--the bound volumes from 1861 to '65. I read the same story that I'm telling you in Harper's. On one occasion, Senator Rouman's father took the boy to the White House to see President Lincoln. In the course of the conversation, President Lincoln picked the boy up and put him on his lap, there in the White House. I'll never forget that. I'm probably the only man living today that met a man who sat on the lap of President Lincoln.

After finishing that second tour of duty in Haiti, in 1930, I was ordered to the Bureau of Medicine and Surgery as a detail officer.

Commander Melhorn: This is a letter from the American Chargé d'Affaires in Port-au-Prince to the Secretary of State, August, 1930.

"Sir: Upon the occasion of departure of Captain Kent C. Melhorn, USN, I have the honor to transmit for the Department's information and files of the Navy Department for inclusion in Dr. Melhorn's service record, several articles from the newspapers praising his work here as director general of the Haitian Department of Public Health. And there is also enclosed a translation of excerpts of these articles. These tributes to Dr. Melhorn express the general feeling in Haiti as regards his work and personality, and are remarkable in view of the usual hostility of the press towards the work of the intervention and American officials generally. It is to be noted that two of these articles are from opposition newspapers, which for years have printed violent and largely unfounded attacks on the American occupation and its officials. Respectfully yours, Stuart Grummon."

Excerpts from newspaper articles, La Presse, July 31, 1930:

"Dr. Melhorn was more than an American citizen, he was a citizen of humanity, and it is in this respect that we send him our sincere congratulations, and the expression of our ardent gratitude for the good which he has known how to achieve for the Haitian people."

In Le Nouvelliste, and this was probably the most violent of the opposition newspapers:

"It is a record to the honor of Dr. Melhorn that he has been able to secure unanimous approval and to obtain, so evidently, mutual support in his sphere of action. This by virtue of a delicate and dominant, rare and personal aptitudes."

Again from an opposition newspaper, Le Temps:

"Everyone, in effect, is unanimous in recognizing that you have done an enormous amount of good, and that you have acted with a disinterestedness which characterizes all noble hearts. You are leaving, your work remains. Patients will long keep the remembrance of your administration of the public health service."

I think it's indicative of the fact that if one did his job, even the opposition would take note of it--that they were people of good will, also.

Q: I'm sure you hated to leave. Or did you feel that you

had done a job well?

Admiral Melhorn: Mrs. Melhorn spoke fluent French and had many friends among the upper-class Haitians, not only because she was a remarkable person, herself, but because of the music. One of her accomplishments was in helping to establish a medical center in the middle of Port-au-Prince. I was anxious to do that because there we could make examinations of servants. We wanted to be sure that the servants going into a home, either an American home or a Haitian home, were disease-free. We established that clinic, and we did a fine piece of work there. If a person passed his exam successfully, we gave her or him a certificate which they could show to their employer. Mrs. Melhorn was a tremendous help, because she did something that never before, and I'm sure never afterwards, had occurred in Haiti. She persuaded the ladies of the upper class to come down and work in that clinic. Now that's a feat. You go into any Latin American country and, by golly, you don't find upper class people doing that. You might today, but in my day you never saw anything like that.

Commander Melhorn: Hasn't this been one of the complaints in the black revolution in this country today, in that there is difficulty getting the upper Negro classes to help?

Admiral Melhorn: Yes.

Kent Melhorn - 4

Q: Well, it's been true in all the Latin American countries, too, that whoever's at the top wants to stay there. The gap between them is so fantastic and they apparently don't care about changing it, and that would be their tragedy.

Admiral Melhorn: The other story that I think might be of some historical interest--because there's history back of this--at the conclusion of the War Between the States in our country, there was a Dr. Lowell from Boston, Massachusetts, who didn't agree with the freeing of the slaves in this country, so he left. He went to Haiti and established himself in the town of Jeremie, where I had picked the doctor to relieve me. While there, he married a Haitian woman, and a grandson of that was a chap named Dr. L'Berrison who was one of the men that I had picked to go to Harvard for this special work under the Rockefeller Foundation. I can prove what I'm saying because I have the book History of Haitian Medicine that carries the documents. Dr. Parsons wrote it up. Dr. Lowell, who was then president of Harvard, would have been greatly interested had he known that in one of his classes at Harvard was a blood relative--a black man.

Q: Do you know whether he did know it or not?

Admiral Melhorn: No, he didn't know it, and I didn't breathe it. The Lowell family doesn't know it to this day, I'm sure, but that's an actual fact.

Q: Then you went back to Washington, I believe, at the end of that tour.

Admiral Melhorn: In 1930, I was ordered to the Bureau of Medicine and Surgery as the detail officer for doctors and dentists, pharmacists. While in that office, one day I received a telephone call with a voice at the other end saying, "Melhorn, how would you like to go to Europe?"

I said, "Oh yea." I thought somebody was pulling my leg.

He said, "I'm serious."

I said, "Who is this?"

He said, "This is Cary Grayson."[*] That was Admiral Grayson, who was the White House physician. He said, "I understand that you've taken care of Senator Swanson."[**]

I said, "Yes, he's been one of my patients."

He said, "The President wants you to go with him to Geneva; he's to be one of the delegates to the disarmament conference in Geneva, and your primary job is to go over there and take care of the old gentleman."[***]

---

[*] Rear Admiral Cary T. Grayson, MC, USN (Retired).
[**] Senator Claude A. Swanson (Democrat-Virginia), who later served as Secretary of the Navy from 1933 to 1939.
[***] The World Disarmament Conference opened in Geneva in February 1932.

So I said, "Yes, I'd be delighted to go to Europe, to Geneva." So within a few days I had orders via the State Department and the Navy Department to become a temporary member of the General Board, which I believe is the most unusual thing in the history of my corps to have a doctor ordered to the General Board of the Navy. So I reported to the State Department and to the General Board, and the admiral in charge at the General Board of the Navy was Admiral Hepburn.* Some of those naval officers on that board later gained great fame in the Navy. One was Commander Tom Kinkaid. Another was Commander Kelly Turner.

Commander Melhorn: Both of whom accompanied you to Geneva.

Admiral Melhorn: Yes. As I say, Admiral Hepburn was the head of our naval delegation. But the overall ranking person in the American delegation was our ambassador to Belgium, Hugh Gibson, a great friend of President Hoover. Mr. Gibson had been one of Mr. Hoover's right-hand men in the relief work that went on in Europe after the war.

Q: Perhaps I misundertood you, but I thought you said you were going to be the doctor to the President?

Admiral Melhorn: To Senator Swanson. I was especially to take care of him.

---

*Rear Admiral Arthur J. Hepburn, USN.

Commander Melhorn: You were really the physician to the American delegation.

Admiral Melhorn: That's what my assignment was.

Commander Melhorn: Senator Swanson was the chairman of the Senate Naval Affairs Committee at the time, and he was one of the heads of the delegation. The other was Miss Mary Woolley, who was the president of Mount Holyoke.*

Admiral Melhorn: My experience at the General Board was just as a silent witness. I sat off in a corner and listened with both ears opened. It was intensely interesting. The principal recollection that I have was the fact that we were under no consideration to sanction the reduction of our cruisers.

Late in January 1932, I departed with the delegation on the steamship President Harding for Geneva. We landed in France and were supplied with a special deluxe train at Le Havre, and taken up to Paris where we spent the night. The next day, boarding the same train, we went on to Geneva. Nothing of any special interest from a doctor's standpoint occurred in Geneva, except that I was landed in the midst of a flu epidemic, and was so busy that I was not able to see anything of Europe until the conclusion of the conference. Then I came out with the family, down through Germany.

---

*Dr. Mary E. Woolley, president of Mount Holyoke College.

Q: Did you sit in on any of the meetings?

Admiral Melhorn: Only as a silent witness.

Q: What did you observe? Any incidents?

Admiral Melhorn: Well, the most interesting observance was to hear the number one Russian delegate, Litvinoff, speak.* When it was announced that he was going to make a speech, the galleries were crowded. He spoke very fluent English, having lived at one time in New York.

Commander Melhorn: He had an English wife, too.

Admiral Melhorn: Yes. One day I had a few moments, and I wanted to attend a meeting of the League of Nations, so I called a taxi and told him to take me to the League of Nations. We went into the main entrance where I wasn't supposed to go, not being a delegate, so I was stopped at the gate, and the guard said, "Délégué?"

I said, "Oui." It was the only French I knew, so I was ushered in down on the main floor. But I quickly got out of there and went back into the gallery. That was the only time I ever exercised my French, but it got me in the main gate.

---

*Maxim Litvinoff.

Kent Melhorn - 49

Q: Did you have any dealings at all with Ambassador Gibson?

Admiral Melhorn: Yes, I did. I helped take care of Mrs. Gibson. In fact, I was quite a busy doctor in Geneva, not only among our own delegates, but among the British. The British didn't have a doctor, so I was helping take care of their people, too. Speaking of Mr. Gibson, reminds me it's always been a favorite drink of mine, and I wondered why they called it Gibson. Some years later I learned that Mr. Gibson, when he went out to a party was very abstemious. He didn't take any liquor, but he would always call for a glass, and he would always tip off the fellow who brought the glass to fill it full of water and put an onion in it. It made it look like liquor, but it was just plain water with an onion. And that's how the name Gibson occurred.

Q: Do you remember what Litvinoff was speaking on--what his topic was?

Commander Melhorn: It was the bombing of Shanghai. This was at the time of the bombardment of the Woosung Forts, the spring of 1932, by the Japanese, the Shanghai incident.

Q: You spoke of Miss Mary Woolley being very much for disarmament. Could you enlarge on that at all?

Kent Melhorn - 5

Admiral Melhorn: Well, she did it in a very nice way but a very demanding way. Of course, her opinion didn't carry any particular weight. A group of American women came over to Geneva to take part in a demonstration before the League of Nations, but they didn't accomplish anything.

Commander Melhorn: Was Miss Woolley a pacifist? Did she want unilateral disarmament?

Admiral Melhorn: Yes.

Q: She wanted us to disarm whether the other nations did or not?

Admiral Melhorn: But of course, nothing ever came of that.

Q: Were there any other people whose names you recall?

Admiral Melhorn: There was a General Strong of the Army, General Simon of the Army. I remember General Simon particularly because he and his wife brought two daughters with them. Mrs. Melhorn was able to get away from Geneva from time to time, and she took Elsa down to Italy, and she had to chaperone these gals. She had kind of a tough time, because they always wanted to go out in a gondola in Venice.

Q: How long were you in Geneva?

Admiral Melhorn: About seven months. Shortly after Mrs. Melhorn and I had gotten planted there in Geneva, we went down to meet our son, Charlie, who had come over to France after finishing school work in Washington. As we were pulling in to the station, we saw him on the car that was heading for Paris. He saw me and jumped off, and I jumped off. He got on my train and I got on his car, and Mrs. Melhorn and I were headed for Paris without Charlie. Well, there wasn't any way to stop those French trains, you couldn't reach up and pull a cord, we had to get off at the first stop which was 50 miles up the line somewhere. We hired a taxi and went back to Le Havre to look for Charlie. He had tried to find the American consul there, but being Sunday, it was closed, but he did meet up with the stationmaster. When we got back to Le Havre, we looked up the stationmaster and told him we had lost our son. It was about that time that the Lindbergh baby matter had occurred, and we were quite concerned.* The stationmaster said, "Oh, you don't have to worry. I know where he is. He's over there in that little restaurant." So we walked over there, and there was Charlie with tears rolling down his face. He'd done the right thing; he'd reported.**

One of the times that I had him with me, when I did get off, he wanted to see some of the old battlefields. So I

---

*The kidnaping in New Jersey of Charles A. Lindbergh, Jr.
**Charles Melhorn was then 13 years old.

took him with me on this trip, and we went around some of these old caves up there--Ypres. He picked up a German helmet with a big spike on it. When we got off the train at Geneva, coming back, there was quite a crowd there, as there always is watching a train arrive. He got off the train with this helmet on and held up his hands and said, "Heil, Hitler!" The whole crowd came down with a roar.

Q: You did start to say that at the end of the conference you had a trip through Europe?

Admiral Melhorn: Well, we went down the Rhine and spent the night at Heidelberg, and watched the Germans drink beer, then came back through Brussels where Mrs. Melhorn had been a student for a couple of years taking special work in piano.

Commander Melhorn: This was in the summer of 1932, and I think the thing that impressed me most about that trip was that we were all traveling on diplomatic passports, which normally exempts you from search and seizure when you cross these borders, and this applied at all but the German borders. We were required to open up just like people traveling on a normal passport, which was certainly a breach of international courtesy and indicative of the attitude of the brown shirts, Hitler having just come into power. That was the summer of '32.

Admiral Melhorn: Yes, the brown shirts were marching up and down the streets there, practicing their drills. Well, I returned to the Bureau of Medicine and Surgery on the 12th of August 1932. A short time after that, I was ordered to the hospital ship Relief as the senior medical officer.

Q: Where was she at the time you went aboard?

Admiral Melhorn: Long Beach. On the 30th of March 1935, I was ordered to the USS Pennsylvania as the fleet medical officer on the staff of the Commander in Chief, U.S. Fleet, Admiral Reeves.[*] Admiral Reeves was quite an exceptional man in this respect--he was a remarkable speaker. He was tall, he was probably the only admiral of his time wearing a beard. It looked quite distinguished and well cropped, and he was in great demand as a speaker, particularly at banquets and things like that. I accompanied him on one occasion when he was invited to speak before the faculty and members of the family at Cal Tech, in Pasadena. We were given a special police escort and we went whizzing up there. I was very curious because I had never heard him speak, but I knew his gift from hearing others speak of it. He had the happy faculty of always interjecting a bit of humor if it became necessary--if he saw people were getting drowsy. To illustrate that, he told this story, which I some years later read repeated in the

---

[*] Admiral Joseph M. Reeves, USN, Commander in Chief U.S. Fleet.

Reader's Digest. He used this in starting off his address that evening at Cal Tech. He said, "When you join the Navy, you always have to be prepared for the unexpected, like the school teacher who wished to illustrate the evils of alcohol to her pupils. She took two glasses and put them on her table. In the first glass she poured water. The second glass, she poured full of whisky. Then she took two earthworms and dropped them in this glass of water, and held it up, and they just wriggled and wriggled and kept on wriggling. Then she took two earthworms and put them in the glass of alcohol, and they wriggled briefly, then dropped dead at the bottom. She turned to the class and said, 'What does that mean to you?' And bright young Johnny held up his hand and said, 'Well, it's just this, Teacher, if you always drink whiskey, you'll never have worms.'"

Q: That's a good story. I think often the stories that men tell are as indicative of the kind of person as some of the more serious things they did. Where was it you served with Admiral Reeves?

Admiral Melhorn: On the Pennsylvania, the flagship of the Pacific Fleet.

Q: And that was in Long Beach then?

Kent Melhorn - 55

Admiral Melhorn: It was all through the Pacific, as far west as Honolulu--Pearl Harbor.

Q: Where was the home port of the Pennsylvania?

Commander Melhorn: Mare Island was the home yard. Long Beach was the homeport.

Admiral Melhorn: At the conclusion of that duty on June 29, 1936, I reported to the naval hospital, San Diego, California, as the executive officer. There the only unpleasant experience I had in my whole 40 years occurred. One day, while I was acting in command, the commanding officer being away on leave, the senior dental officer came to me and said, "I have to have help."

I said, "Help for what?"

He said, "I'm being bombarded by dependents who are demanding dental care. I don't seem to be able to stop them."

So I said, "Send them over to my office; maybe I can help." It was contrary to the Navy regulations at that time to take care of dependents for dentistry.

Q: Yes. It still is.

Admiral Melhorn: Yes. So a day or so later, into my office

came Admiral Webb, of my corps.* He was the inspector general of the medical department up and down the West Coast, and he said, "I understand that I can't get dental care for my wife here."

I thought he was probably joking to see how I would reply. I said, "Yes, Admiral, that's correct."

He said, "Well, the Surgeon General has assured me that she can receive dental care."

Then I saw that he was in earnest, and I said, "Well, Admiral, the Surgeon General didn't tell this hospital about that. I know nothing about it, and furthermore, as you know, it's contrary to Navy regulation."

Well, I had him. He stomped out of my office. I can still see him, mad as can be. I knew something was going to happen. A few days later, he was ordered back to Washington to be on a selection board, and when he returned, he called me up to his office. He said, "You're being detached."

I said, "Well, I'm surprised. Where am I going?"

He said, "You're going to go up to Long Beach and be in charge of the naval dispensaries at Long Beach and San Pedro. How do you like it?"

I said, "Admiral, of course I'm disappointed to be leaving here. I haven't been here very long, but I've never objected to orders; I've never asked for orders. I go where I'm sent and do the best I can. If that's where I'm to go, I'll do

---

*Rear Admiral Ulys Robert Webb, MC, USN.

the best I can there." So we moved and found a nice place to live in Long Beach.

Q: How could a man, knowing you were doing exactly what you were supposed to be doing, take that action?

Admiral Melhorn: Because he knew I had him on the spot, and he didn't know how to get out of it, other than to stomp his feet and see that I was detached. After I'd been at Long Beach, it wasn't very long, the Surgeon General came out on an inspection--Admiral Rossiter.[*] Shortly after he got in the office he said, "Melhorn, what was wrong down there in San Diego?"

I said, "You ask for the story, I'll tell it to you." And I repeated it. And I said, "Furthermore, Admiral Webb told me that you had sanctioned dental service for his wife."

He kind of flushed for a moment and said, "That's a damned lie." I'm not sure if it was a damned lie or not. Anyway, that's the only unpleasant experience I ever had.

Q: Well, to have it react badly for you is a shame.

Admiral Melhorn: As it turned out, the incident became known throughout my corps. I didn't blab it around, but friends who knew about it, particularly Parsons and the crowd down

---

[*]Rear Admiral Perceval S. Rossiter, MC, USN.

there who were on my side, apparently had spread the word, so it never hurt me a bit, because I had stood up for what was right and rode the wave. I thought my career was ruined to be suddenly detached like that, but it turned out otherwise.

Q: Was Ray Batchley your CO?

Admiral Melhorn: No, my commanding officer was Captain Porter, but he wasn't there at the time.*

Q: How long were you in Long Beach and San Pedro?

Admiral Melhorn: Almost two years. One of the days while I was there at my office at Long Beach, my phone rang, and a voice at the other end introduced himself as Colonel So-and-so. He said, "I'm living in an apartment here in Long Beach, down on the waterfront, and I made a discovery which I would like to report." Why he called me, I don't know. I guess he had been long retired and knew that there was a government official in my office, so I asked him to come in. He came in and said, "I've been noticing a car out my window; it's headed so they could look out at the ocean, and my curiosity has been aroused because I've seen this car frequently. This morning I took my field glasses and looked out the window to see what was going on in that car, and in it I saw a Jap, and he was working

---

*Captain Frederick E. Porter, MC, USN.

some dials up on the dash. It occurred to me that that's a matter that ought to be investigated, so that's why I've come to tell you about it."

I said, "That certainly could be very important. Maybe he's trying to find out some radio stuff." I thanked him, and he left. I immediately got in touch with the naval intelligence people in Long Beach, and they came in right away.

That's the last I heard of it, but a couple of weeks later, the same colonel called me again and said, "I have something more to tell you." So in he came again. He said, "This morning that same car and the same Jap drove up to the usual place, working that stuff, and all of a sudden, another car drove in behind him, and out stepped two gentlemen who went over and opened this Jap's car door and took him out, and that's the last I've seen of him."

Q: So it had been effective.

Admiral Melhorn: Yes. So anyway, I had something to do with the arrest of a Japanese spy.

Then in April 1939, I received a dispatch from Admiral Richardson, who was in the Navy Department in Washington, stating that he was being ordered to command the battleships, Pacific Fleet, with the assurance of President Roosevelt that within a few months he would be ordered to be Commander in Chief, Pacific Fleet.* Admiral Richardson requested that I join his staff for the next tour of duty. I had known Admiral Richardson from the days when he was a lieutenant in charge of a torpedo boat back in the Atlantic, when I was, in those days, on the _Dixie_. Of course, my reply was, "Aye, aye, Sir." That's how I happened to have a second tour as the fleet medical officer, Pacific Fleet. It's the only time that's ever occurred. Admiral Richardson was a wonderful man. He was especially beloved by everybody--enlisted men and his officers. He had very firm ideas about our battleships en masse, and he was wanting to get them out of Pearl Harbor. He wanted to bring them out into the ocean for maneuvering purposes and not keep them in Pearl Harbor. He made his wishes known, of course, at the Navy Department, and he was directed to return to Washington temporarily for a conference with the President. He left the ship for that purpose. I happened to be on the quarterdeck, walking up and down, when he returned. As he came up on deck, he saw me and gave me the high sign to follow him. I went down to his cabin with him and he said, "Well, Melhorn, my days are numbered. I'm going to be detached. I've had a very strenuous time talking to the President, and he doesn't agree with my views about the battleships, and I'm being detached. The President also asked me to recommend my successor, and I recommended Admiral Kimmel."** Well, that was that.

---

*Admiral James O. Richardson, USN.
**Admiral Husband E. Kimmel, USN.

Kent Melhorn - 61

Q: The headquarters had moved out to Pearl by this time, had they not?

Admiral Melhorn: Yes. So Admiral Kimmel shortly afterwards came aboard, and Admiral Richardson was relieved. But before Admiral Kimmel took over, he asked, would I remain? I thanked him for the compliment of asking me to remain, but I had been at sea, with the experience on the Relief, almost three years, and I wanted to get ashore and get, possibly, command of a naval hospital. So I turned it down. In fact, practically all Admiral Richardson's staff, with one or two exceptions, left at the same time the admiral did.

Q: What was the atmosphere in the fleet in those days? This was late 1940, wasn't it? Was it one of apprehension, or concern, or do you recall?

Admiral Melhorn: It was concern. As a doctor man, you sometimes learn things that other folks don't. I never made it a point to try to pick up information, but sometimes I couldn't help but gather it. I remember one day, walking up and down the deck on the Pennsylvania with Captain Taffinder, chief of staff, and he told me that one of our destroyers had picked up, due to the sounding device, a foreign submarine that was passing up and down in front of Pearl Harbor entrance.*

---

*Captain Sherwoode A. Taffinder, USN.

Kent Melhorn - 6

They suspected that it was a Jap. So we put some of our destroyers with their sounding equipment over this, and put one of our subs ahead of it to see if there was anything to this kind of a maneuver, and it turned out there was. In other words, it was known that there was going to be trouble. Of course, those things were never discussed openly, but I knew it wouldn't be long before we were going to get into a war.

Q: You remember any other anecdotes or stories from that period?

Admiral Melhorn: Well, while the Pennsylvania was in San Francisco one weekend, I got on the phone and called up a nephew of mine, who was a student at Stanford, about to graduate in mechanical engineering. His name is Frank Lindsay.* He's now the president of Itek Corporation, in Boston. So I said, "Frank, come down and have dinner with me."

He said, "Sure, I'd be glad to." He came, and I found out during the course of dinner, he hadn't the faintest idea about military service, Army, Navy or Marine Corps. He wasn't interested. So I asked him to come into my room.

I said, "Frank, I want to have a talk with you. I happen to know we are about to get into a war, and my advice to you, when you go back to Stanford, you enlist in the Army ROTC, so when we get into this war you won't be peeling potatoes

---

*Franklin A. Lindsay, president of Itek Corporation, 1962-1975; chairman of board, 1975-1981.

somewhere in a camp. You come in as a commissioned officer." He thought it over, and he did just that. He was a brilliant student. He didn't tell me that; I learned that later. On graduation, he was ordered to the General Staff, Army, in Washington, as a subordinate, of course, and his job took him all around the country looking into places where they make ammunition and guns--things like that. He got kind of tired of that. Meantime, I'd been ordered to Brooklyn in charge of the Naval Medical Supply Depot.

One day in Brooklyn, the phone rang, and Frank was on the line. He said, "Can I come and have lunch with you? I can't tell you any more about it now." So he came to our apartment and had lunch, and said, "I'm on my way. I can't tell you where I'm going, but I have orders." We were very curious. Where in the world was he going? Next we heard from him in about two months. He was Teheran, and he was helping push up trucks--jeep, ammunition, what have you--into Russia under the Lend-Lease Program. He got tired of that, and he wasn't getting into the war, so he asked for something more active, and he was sent to Palestine to take a course in parachute school, to learn to jump out of a plane. When he graduated from that, he got orders to Rome. One night, with three or four others, he was ordered to enplane, and he was dropped at night in Yugoslavia, where he spent almost a year living in caves and tunnels, making friends with the partisans, and one jump ahead of the Nazis. That's where he met Tito. Well, when the armistice came, he was still alive and received orders to become the acting American minister to Yugoslavia until the State Department could get a man over there. He carried that off very well.

When he returned to the States, he went to the Harvard Business School, and graduated there, and then was given a job with one of these big management engineering firms in New York. This firm was requested to go to Boston to make a study of the Itek Corporation and their operations and so forth. They did, and came up with a report which the board of directors liked. The board of directors wanted to get rid of their president who wasn't doing very well with that company, so they asked Frank to come over and be the vice president, with assurances that if everything went well, he would be the president of the Itek Corporation. I always felt that I had something to do with that young man's career.

Q: You had a sense of what was going to happen. I know you influenced Charlie in his actions, too.

Admiral Melhorn: My next assignment was at the Naval Medical Supply Depot in Brooklyn.

Q: You went there directly from the duty with Admiral Richardson

Admiral Melhorn: That's right. My job there was to see that medical, dental, sanitary hospital supplies were sent all over the world. And get them there in time. Now that included Russia under the Lend-Lease Program. It was quite an active assignment.

Q: I'm sure it had grown enormously in size, hadn't it?

Admiral Melhorn: We had to take over a great big plant in Jersey, because we didn't have enough room there on Sand Street. About once a week I had to go to Washington. The Surgeon General would call me. He was there at the White House, of course, as the White House physician as well as Surgeon General, and he would see that big board every morning and know what was coming up. He would call me to give me two or three weeks' notice on shipments that had to be such-and-such a place on time. On one of these occasions, I called up Admiral Richardson just to say hello--he was retired and living out on Connecticut Avenue--and he said, "Well, come on out and have dinner with me."

So I did and had a very pleasant evening with the admiral and Mrs. Richardson. In the course of the dinner I said, "Admiral, I'm going to ask you a very personal question. If it's out of order, just consider that I haven't asked the question."

That aroused his curiosity, and he said, "What is it?"

I said, "The whole Navy and the whole country was wondering what was your reaction on the morning of December 7th?" Without a moment's hesitation, he said, "I can answer that. I made a prayer for two things. First for the success of our armed forces and second that I keep my mouth shut." And to this day he has kept his mouth shut. But I happen to know that after his death, there will be a book released which will tell the story of Pearl Harbor from Admiral Richardson's side. But not until after he dies.*

Q: He had wanted, as I understand, the fleet to be back on the West Coast?

Admiral Melhorn: Not so much on the West Coast, but maneuvering in the Pacific. Of course, they would have to go back to the West Coast for repairs, but not a whole group of battleships en masse like there were in Pearl Harbor.

Q: So many things about that, in retrospect, were peculiar, it's difficult to understand. That especially tied to the comment he made to you when he returned from Washington.

Admiral Melhorn: My assignment to the Naval Medical Supply Depot began on the 1st of February 1941. I was also assigned

---

*Admiral Richardson's memoir wound up being published shortly before his death in 1974: On the Treadmill to Pearl Harbor (Washington: U.S. Government Printing Office, 1973).

as the chief of material division, Bureau of Medicine and Surgery in the Navy Department. While on that duty there in Naval Medical Supply Depot, I had an interesting experience with Mayor Hague of Jersey City.* The Surgeon General had told me that he wanted me to look around New York and see if there was available another place for a naval hospital. The President had been told that Mr. Hague would loan the Jersey City hospital to the Navy for the duration, and we were to go and have a look at it. So I took some officers with me, and we went over and met Mayor Hague and were taken around over the place. It's a sizable structure they had there and quite well equipped, and something the Navy could have used. He was a strange sort of fellow. He was one of these glad-handers--slap you on the back type of fellow. I was a little suspicious of him. So after inspecting the place for about two days, I and the group of officers with me asked to have a look at the books as to what this thing was costing to maintain a day. He wouldn't let us see the books. No sir. So I asked no questions, and we left. I told the Surgeon General, "Hands off that place. We'll have to look for something else." And he agreed with me.

Q: Was he just trying to get rid of a hot potato?

Admiral Melhorn: Apparently. He didn't want anybody to look

---

*Frank Hague, notorious as a political manipulator, was mayor of Jersey City from 1917 to 1947.

at those books. So when the word got around that the Navy wasn't going to take over the hospital, I was besieged with telephone calls and visits from reporters in Jersey City wanting to know what in the world happened. Of course, I never told them. I said they had to get any information they wanted from Washington. That was my only experience with a dyed-in-the-wool politician.

Q: I guess he really was a true one.

Admiral Melhorn: I know one of the places we inspected in connection with that was a big dock that ran out into the river. We wanted to see the condition of that dock, so we went down to the shoreline, and as we passed, the people would get down on their knees--sort of saluting, as though he were a king of some kind.

Q: I've never heard of that in this country. How did he react to that?

Admiral Melhorn: Oh, he liked it. It was all votes for him.
   That's about it. I was promoted to rear admiral on September 15, 1942.

Q: Where were you on Pearl Harbor Day?

Admiral Melhorn: I was in Brooklyn.

Q: How did you react? How did you feel when you heard the news?

Admiral Melhorn: I was expecting it. I was out at dinner with some friends in Brooklyn when the news came over the air. The dinner was immediately called off, and I rushed back to the office. All my staff had heard about it, and they were there. We put into effect the orders that you do in an emergency in wartime. That was that.

It was interesting duty. Particularly those who are in the business, like pharmaceutical houses, instrument houses.

Q: You were really in the business world. In a big way, too.

Admiral Melhorn: Oh yes, we were spending over a million dollars a day there at one time.

Q: Did you have all civilians working for you?

Admiral Melhorn: Yes, a large part. We had about 200 employees there, and then I had an executive officer and a naval medical officer. I also had a group of pharmacists and chemists.

Secretary Forrestal had instituted the idea of having a group of management engineers visit various naval installations in the country, and such a group came up to us.* I took quite an interest in them, because we had never had a scientific study of our plant made, and there were many things about it that I didn't like but I didn't know how to solve.

Q: After all, you hadn't been trained to be a businessman.

Admiral Melhorn: No, and when they came up with the report, I read it with a great bit of interest, and I phoned the Surgeon General and said, "I have a request to make. There's a man on this group that studied me whom I respect very highly, and I'd like to have him on my staff up here." Well, it appealed to the Surgeon General, and he apparently told Secretary Forrestal about it, and it quite pleased him.

Q: Well, it would. That was certainly an intelligent approach.

Admiral Melhorn: So this young man was assigned to us.

Q: Was he Navy?

Admiral Melhorn: No, civilian. He was given a temporary commission. I hear from him every Christmas now. He and

---

*Under Secretary of the Navy James V. Forrestal.

his wife were great friends of Bennett Cerf of Random House. His wife had been secretary to him.

Q: That is really a good lesson that anyone could well learn-- that if you're inspected, and if there's anything about it at all to say, "I'd like to hire that man." I'd never heard that before, but it's a very good gimmick, I might say.

Admiral Melhorn: Well, that's the same thing that happened to my nephew, Frank Lindsay.

Q: Exactly. Maybe he learned it from you. Then you became rear admiral in 1942, and then you retired in '46. Were you at the Medical Supply Depot all that time?

Admiral Melhorn: Yes.

Q: That was a long tour.

Admiral Melhorn: Yes, five years.

Q: I'm sure that when they got someone in there, they weren't going to take a chance of changing it. You said that later you were going to discuss the various campaign medals that you had.

Kent Melhorn - 7

Admiral Melhorn: While in duty at the Naval Medical Supply Depot in Brooklyn, I had requested that an officer from the British Navy be assigned to my office, someone familiar with medical supplies for the British Navy. So a young man was assigned, a chief pharmacist, I think. He turned out to be quite good, so I was able to be of considerable help to the Royal Navy through him, and after the war, after I was retired, I received a commendation. I was made an honorary commander of the British Empire.

Q: This is interesting as a citation, and it makes you the honorary commander of the military division of the most excellent order of the British Empire, and states that you rendered most valuable aid and cooperation in the supply of medical store to the Royal Navy bases and Royal naval ships which were refitting or commissioning in the United States. That's something special, isn't it? Along with that, the medals that you hold, I would mention the service medal, and you say that was just for a small skirmish in Mexico?

Admiral Melhorn: Somewhere there on the West Coast. I don't even remember what it was.

Q: And the Dominican campaign medal, we've talked about. The Marine Corps Expeditionary Medal, and the Victory Medal,

West Indies clasp, and Bronze Star, and the Haitian campaign medal, the Haitian Medal of Militaire, the Medal of Honor and Merit from the Haitian Government for 1930 and 1936.

Admiral Melhorn: Then I received the Legion of Merit.

Q: The Legion of Merit was from Vice Admiral Louis Denfeld for Admiral Melhorn's duty as medical officer in charge of the Naval Medical Supply Depot in Brooklyn, and the commendation from Josephus Daniels dated November 23, 1916 is also something to treasure, because it speaks of his "bravery, courage and devotion to duty. On the firing line, where the likelihood of casualties was greatest, surgeon Melhorn was always to be found and his cheering manner under trying conditions was a comfort to those with whom he came in contact. The efficiency, courage, and devotion to duty displayed by the officers and enlisted men of the medical corps on duty with the expeditionary forces in Santo Domingo meet with the hearty appreciation and commendation of the major general commandant, and it is strongly recommended that appropriate entries be made in the official records of these officers."

That's nice to have from Josephus Daniels, isn't it? Then you have the letter from James Forrestal on his retirement.

Admiral Melhorn: I had a personal letter.

Kent Melhorn - 7

Q: Yes. It's a very nice letter. It speaks specifically for the fact that you had faithfully and efficiently served and participated in two great wars and witnessed many advancement in the morale, strength, and efficiency of the Navy, and must have the satisfaction of knowing that you have contributed to the accomplishment of these results. That's also a nice letter--a memorable one from Secretary Forrestal.

That pretty well covers your military career, but I wanted to put in the record that Mrs. Melhorn, of whom you speak in such lovely terms--where did you meet her, and when were you married?

Admiral Melhorn: Mrs. Melhorn and I were second cousins. I first met her in a public school in my home town in Ohio. I had been a bad boy in school, and the teacher sent me out in the hall to think over my sins. When I arrived in the hall, there was a young lady who had been a bad girl in class. This was the third grade in public school. That's where we met.

Q: And when were you married, Admiral?

Admiral Melhorn: I was married in Philadelphia in 1908.

Q: And you had two children, I know. A son, Charles, who

Kent Melhorn - 75

is here today. When was he born?

Admiral Melhorn: You'll have to ask him.

Q: And your daughter is younger or older?

Admiral Melhorn: She's older. She's married to Admiral Bird.*

Q: Admiral Bird, who is still the commanding officer at the naval station at Long Beach. And he has a beautiful home, as I mentioned in the beginning of the interview. I've enjoyed this, and I know the Institute will appreciate the effort and detail and study which you have in preparing for the interview. I think it's just remarkable, and you've had, certainly, unusual duty for an officer in the medical corps.

Admiral Melhorn: I enjoyed it very much. If I had my life to live over again, I would do the same thing. I never have been in private practice and never wanted to be. I wanted to join the Navy and spend my life in the Navy, and I have never taken any state board examinations for private practice. Of course, I'm privileged under the Navy regulations to respond for humanitarian reasons if they can't get a doctor, and sometimes I have responded.

---

*Rear Admiral Horace V. Bird, USN. He and Elsa Melhorn were married in 1936.

Kent Melhorn - 7

Q: Have you since retired?

Admiral Melhorn: Yes, here. I've done what I could. Emergencies like automobile accidents and things like that.

Q: In the town of Julian?

Admiral Melhorn: And the countryside. But I don't do that any longer, because I've learned that try as you will, sometimes you might make a mistake, and you can be sued for malpractice. So I'm not responding to calls any more.

Q: You made that decision, I'm sure, based on experience and wisdom of your years.

Admiral Melhorn: These courts, in a malpractice suit, can take everything you own away from you. You have to carry very, very heavy insurance, and all doctors do in active practice.

Q: I hope that preparing for the interview and the interview itself has been of some satisfaction to you.

Admiral Melhorn: It's nice to have this meeting with you and have my son here to help out with this.

Q: Yes, he's been helpful. I'm going to do something that

the Institute doesn't know about. I think it will be unique in their records. Your son is also a naval officer, and I'm going to interview him now, and I'm sure this will be the only father-son taped history in the library of the Institute. I'm sure they will appreciate it. But thank you very much for your excellent and fine interview.

Admiral Melhorn: I've enjoyed having you come to my home.

Q: It's been a pleasure, and thank you so much.

Interview with Commander Charles M. Melhorn, U.S. Navy (Retired)
Place: Rear Admiral Kent C. Melhorn's home, Julian, California
Date: 15 February 1970
Subject: Biography
Interviewer: Commander Etta-Belle Kitchen

Q: This is the first opportunity I've had to do an interview with a father and son, both of whom are retired naval officers. I've persuaded Commander Melhorn to tell us of his Navy career. I want to begin by saying good morning and thank you very much for doing this, and to ask you what was your background for coming into the Navy besides having a Navy father?

Commander Melhorn: Well, I think that was precisely it--having a Navy father. In 1940 I had graduated from UCLA in liberal arts and had gone to the Chilean Andes with a view toward making a career of skiing down there--skiing was just coming into South America. While there at the resort of Portillo, this was in the summer of 1940, I received a cable from my father in Honolulu. He was at that time on the staff of Admiral Richardson. The cable was to the effect that there was going to be a war, and come home and get in it. So I packed my gear, and had enough money for steerage passage home on the Grace liner. I came back, and in September 1940, I joined the Navy as an apprentice seaman in the "90-day wonder" V-7 program, and came in that way.

Q: What was your uniform?

Commander Melhorn: The uniform was one suit of undress blues. The ship to which I was assigned was the New York. Unfortunately we didn't get to sea until quite late because she had thrown a wheel someplace and was back in the Norfolk Navy Yard getting a new one installed. This was termed "the dry-dock cruise." We didn't get out until the last part. My outstanding recollection of the thing is that with my one suit of undress blues--this was for work and also for what liberty we got--I had many friends in the Norfolk area but when I would show up to see them in my suit of undress blues, I was some sort of pariah. They wouldn't have anything to do with me.

From the New York, I went to the Naval Academy for the three months' course. We were the first and last class of D.V.G.--deck volunteer general--officers to go through the Naval Academy. Our impact was less than pleasing to the rest of the brigade.

Q: How many were there of you?

Commander Melhorn: About 600 of us. They had graduated the regular class of 1941 six months early to make room for us, 4th battalion wing in Bancroft Hall.

Charles Melhorn - 8

Q: So you really are an Annapolis graduate? Or a graduate from Annapolis?

Commander Melhorn: Yes, to whatever degree. The one thing that made us really unpopular with the rest of the brigade of regular midshipmen was not so much the fact that we were going to come in and in three months we would rank them and be senior to them, but I think the thing that really stuck in their craw was that when they vacated the 4th battalion wing to make room for us, they also renovated all the bunks and installed innerspring mattresses, whereas the brigade was still sleeping on straw pallets, and this they could not accept.

Q: I can appreciate a little of their feeling.

Commander Melhorn: Yes. So most of us graduated in May of 1941, and the deal was that we were permitted to go on active duty if the offer was made by the Navy Department. The options were all with the Navy Department as to whether or not, on being commissioned in the Naval Reserve, we would take active duty. The offer was made, and most of us then took active duty and came back to an armed guard school right there at the Naval Academy, with the idea of going aboard the various merchant ships that had been outfitted for the transatlantic convoy work. The opportunity came while I was there to join the fleet in an old World War I four-piper division, and I

went to the Gregory. My division had been converted to the fast destroyer transports--they had taken out the forward fire room and made a troop space out of it. We carried the 1st battalion of the 5th Marines, which was Merritt Edson's outfit and which later became the 1st Marine Raider Battalion.*
Gregory was my first ship.

Q: Where did you take them?

Commander Melhorn: We mainly operated on the Atlantic seaboard and opened up the New River area. We were the first ships to go down there. It was just an opened expanse of beach--there were no facilities whatsoever. This later became the Marine Base there at Camp Lejeune. At that time I was riding Colhoun, another ship in the division. My first skipper on the Gregory was Captain Brown who later became skipper of the Missouri when she went aground in the mud.** Then I went over to the Colhoun, and later on in 1941 we were suddenly alerted and went roaring up to Quantico to pick up Marines, and headed out for Martinique to neutralize the French carrier Bearn, which was in Martinique and which posed a threat to the canal. Our orders were to take the ship and neutralize it. About

---

*Lieutenant Colonel Merritt A. "Red Mike" Edson, USMC.
**Lieutenant Commander William D. Brown, USN, who was commanding officer of the USS Missouri when she ran aground near Hampton Roads in January 1950.

three days out we suddenly received word that diplomacy had accomplished what we had set out to do.

Q: What was your job aboard ship then?

Commander Melhorn: I was the boat officer. We were diverted to Miami for a couple of weeks for R and R, which was quite a welcome turn for us because we had been to such garden spots as Wilmington, North Carolina; Cape Fear; Jacksonville, North Carolina--real holes. So we were glad to go.

Q: What time of year would that have been? Coming toward fall?

Commander Melhorn: Coming toward fall. Pearl Harbor found us back in Norfolk, and then we were doing mostly coastal work--convoying to Bermuda, convoying to New York right after the war. Early 1942 we left Edson's battalion and were ordered around to the West Coast to pick up the 2nd Marine Raider Battalion which was Evans F. Carlson's outfit training on Kearney Mesa.* The word was that we were to pick them up here and take Attu. That was the luckiest thing in the world that that fell through, because as I recall the Army poured something short of a division into Attu and had quite a time doing it.

---

*Lieutenant Colonel Evans F. Carlson, USMC.

Charles Melhorn - 83

Q: It was so cold up there.

Commander Melhorn: We wouldn't have fared very well with one battalion of Marines. Instead we took the 2nd Marine Raider Battalion out to Honolulu, and right after the battle of Midway they were split, and part of them went to Midway on garrison duty for the island after the battle. Back here in San Diego they were training out on Jack's farm at Kearney Mesa and all the boat officers were sent ashore to train with them. I got a firsthand look at the Carlson-style Marines which were a style all of their own. Jimmy Roosevelt was the second in command, and it was a most unorthodox outfit.* Every night Carlson--I'm sure because of his experience with the Chinese 19th Route Army which he accompanied. I believe he resigned his commission in Shanghai after the Shanghai incident in 1932--he was on duty with the Marines out there, resigned, and then spent months with the Chinese 19th Route Army.

Q: The ones that went north?

Commander Melhorn: This particular Army group was with Chiang Kai-shek in Central China during the period 1933-1935 when he was trying to suppress his Chinese bandits, namely Mao. Then the 19th Route Army also participated in the Fukien revolt,

---

*Major James Roosevelt, USMCR, son of the President.

Charles Melhorn - 8

I believe in 1933. Carlson was in all this business and when he came back into the Marine Corps, he was thoroughly indoctrinat in Chinese techniques, particularly in military matters of infiltration.

Q: Guerrilla tactics?

Commander Melhorn: Guerrilla tactics. He was a past master at this sort of thing, but every night down at Jack's farm at Kearney Mesa we would have a political indoctrination which amounted to "Why are we fighting? What are the political objectives?" It was here, of course, that the word "gung ho" came into the language.

Q: What's your philosophical approach to that? Good or bad?

Commander Melhorn: Well, at the time Ensign Melhorn was completely apolitical. I just sat up there with the rest. I have some different ideas on it now.

When we were with the battalion down here on Kearney Mesa, there were other Marine observers from the line Marine units, and we would all be stumping along at the rear of the column on these forced marches that we were on, and we marched all night and all day all over the area down there on various field problems. There was nothing but grousing going on in the rear ranks as to Carlson's way of doing things, which was certainly not the accepted Marine concept of how to fight. This impressed me in that I took from that that Carlson wouldn't be too popular among the line of the Marines. And I think that was borne out. We did not take Carlson's outfit into combat because in the meantime, Edson's outfit had been sent down to Samoa and from there, as I recall, they had gone to Noumea. In July of 1942 we went into Noumea.

Q: How did you get from Kearney Mesa to Noumea?

Commander Melhorn: We steamed with the division out to Honolulu and then on down to the Fijis and then into the New Caledonia chain.

Q: Was that preparatory for the Solomons?

Commander Melhorn: It was preparatory for the Guadalcanal campaign, and the forces were marshaling down there. We were steaming independently.

Q: Your ship went alone?

Commander Melhorn: That is the division--the four-ship division. At this time we were Colhoun, Gregory, Little, and Manley.

Stringham and McKean were on other duty. We picked up Edson's outfit, and our objective was the Tulagi side of the Guadalcanal landings. We didn't join up with the force, the assaulting force, until late July of 1942. The general rendezvous for the Guadalcanal force was south and east of the Fijis, and then we went to Koro Island in the Fijis, a small island, and proceeded to rehearse the entire Guadalcanal operation. I spent, because of the nature of the reefs and the nature of my work as the boat officer in there, we were on and off the reefs--I spent the better part of three days in the water and picked up a terrible cold which was to develop into pneumonia the night before the Tulagi landings. So I did not actually make the landings.

Q: Haven't you ever felt that you were fortunate?

Commander Melhorn: Well, we didn't lose much in the landings. I felt that I was quite fortunate at the time because we had our skipper, George Madden, "Mutt" Madden--his class was '31 at the Naval Academy.* He was an old Asiatic sailor from the early days with the Asiatic Fleet, and apparently they had a uniform, a service uniform out there that was almost equivalent of our service white. Captain Madden had always had a soft spot in his heart for this particular uniform, and he decreed the morning of the Guadalcanal landings that

---

*Lieutenant Commander George B. Madden, USN, commanding officer of the USS Colhoun.

the uniform of the day for officers was going to be service whites.

Q: So they could shoot at you better.

Commander Melhorn: Well, I looked at him like he was demented. I said, "Captain, I'm the boat officer. These Marines are all camouflaged to the hilt, the ship is camouflaged even to the extent of netting on the sides, the crew are wearing dungarees, and I'm riding the boat. If I go in there in a suit of whites I'm going to look like Napoleon coming up there, and everybody in the place is going to be shooting at me."

He said, "No, you're an officer on this ship, and the uniform for officers is service whites, so you will go in service whites." Well, luckily, I came down with pneumonia that night, and George Lewis, who was the communicator, had to take the boats in, in white. But the Japanese tactic at Tulagi was to allow all the boats to come in. Over at Gavutu and Tanambogo the passage was contested on the way in, but the Tulagi strategy was to let us land, so I probably would have made it all right. At least George Lewis made it.

Q: Didn't he send you over in dress whites to pick up the mail?

Commander Melhorn: This was just before. We had gone way

over the horizon--<u>Atlanta</u> was over there. I believe Admiral Norman Scott was flying his flag in her then, and she flashed over a message that she had mail for us.* We were out in the open sea and Captain Madden said, "All right, Melhorn, go over and get the mail." So I jumped into the Higgins boat, and we started to lower away, and he said, "Where are you going?"

I said, "I'm going to get the mail."

He said, "Not like that, you're not going. Go in and get into whites." So I went across about 15 miles of open sea wearing whites, and completely drenched. As we pulled up alongside this cruiser, we provided a lot of raised eyebrows and mirth and merriment for those on the bridge. I remember all the fingers pointing down at me and the watch officers and staff officers were doubled up on the deck, seeing this idiot coming alongside in whites.

The Guadalcanal landings went off, as far as we were concerned, without a hitch. I was down below in my bunk. We didn't have a doctor aboard, and this thing had been diagnosed as "cat fever with respiratory complications," and I was pretty sick down in my bunk while all this was going on. We were under one fast, heavy air raid by a group of Bettys. I heard the large-caliber antiaircraft guns from the surrounding ships begin to fire and figured they were still pretty far off,

---

*Rear Admiral Norman Scott, USN, Commander Task Group 62.4, who was killed by Japanese gunfire the night of 13 November 1942 while in the <u>Atlanta</u>.

but when I heard our own .50-caliber machine guns start to go, I figured they were pretty close and I had better get up on deck. So I went up on deck just in time to see one of these Bettys being shot down pretty close aboard. It was an extremely low-level attack, and when they were shot down they only dropped about 15 feet and skidded quite a ways through the water. These three Japs had crawled out on the wing and were standing there, and we steamed along, just nosed into the wreck which was still afloat and tried to get them aboard, and they brandished pistols. They refused to come aboard, whereupon the captain backed off. We were going to make another approach to them, or lower a boat to go get them. In the meantime another destroyer had gone in, and there was a brief exchange of gunfire, and by the time we got back, the three Japs were dead in the water. As the ship went by, very, very slowly, our crew--our fine, civilized, Jack Armstrong-type American boys were on the fantail with the boathooks, and they fished those corpses up out of the water and were pounding on them with rifle butts in order to get souvenirs like gold teeth. When I think today of the horror that goes through the country at the thought of any such thing as the My Lai massacre in Vietnam, I say we have short memories, because I found my own people doing something on the order of the same thing. Certainly it was pretty savage thing to do. These things are fairly routine in war.

After we lost the four cruisers on the night of the 9th of August, there was a general bug-out. Admiral Turner, now bereft of any surface support, just simply had to get the transports out, so we all skedaddled and were heading back down south for the Hebrides.* In the meantime, I was getting no better fast, and Captain Madden finally sent a message over to the McCawley that they had a sick officer aboard and requested instructions and suggested a transfer since we had no doctor. The message came back almost immediately from the McCawley that there was no time to make a transfer. Then about four hours later another message came in from the McCawley. The transfer would be made at once. This was signed, Admiral Turner. Admiral Turner had been an old friend of the family. He and my father had been together in Geneva in 1932 at the disarmament conference and had been rather close ever since. What I think happened was that Admiral Turner finally leafed through the dispatches, saw my name as the sick officer and thought if there was a chance they had better get me aboard. So we nosed alongside, and they had me up on the bow of the Colhoun in a stokes stretcher, lashed in. The big transports had had to get out of Guadalcanal so quickly that they were still half loaded and still had their great big unloading tackle in the rigging in the booms, and what came over to hoist me was a great big tank hook which must have weighed

---

*Rear Admiral Richmond Kelly Turner, USN, Commander Amphibious Force South Pacific. Embarked in the McCawley, he was amphibious task force commander for the Guadalcanal-Tulagi landings.

300 pounds, and with the McCawley wallowing and the Colhoun pitching, this jumbo hook was a pretty wild thing up there.

Q: It's a wonder it didn't kill you.

Commander Melhorn: At the crucial moment, just as they were about to try and capture this thing, we had about five sailors up there trying to hang on to it, the wheel ropes of the Colhoun broke, and we had to sheer out. I could look over there, and I saw Admiral Turner standing on one of the upper decks watching this operation and shaking his head. The next morning we tried it again, and I was transferred to the McCawley, and from there in Noumea to the Solace, I think it was--anyway to a hospital ship. We went down to Auckland, New Zealand, to a mobile hospital, and I recovered there in an SOQ, which was an open ward with all the wounded from Astoria, Vincennes, Quincy and Canberra.* I spent a couple of months in New Zealand and was getting ready to, I thought, go home, because in the meantime Colhoun had been sunk and all of the survivors had gone back. But when my orders came through in New Zealand, I was ordered back to ComSoPac for further assignment.**

I took off on a transport which made the grand tour of

---

*SOQ--sick officers' quarters. The four ships listed are the four cruisers Commander Melhorn mentions earlier as having been sunk on 9 August.
**ComSoPac--Commander South Pacific Force, who was Vice Admiral Robert L. Ghormley, with headquarters at Noumea, New Caledonia.

Tongatabu, the Fijis, the Hebrides, and we went every place but Noumea trying to get to Noumea. We finally got into Efate, and it was there a request came in for volunteers to go out to Vireo. The Vireo was one of the old bird-class minesweeps which had been towing--this was in October of 1942 and things were extremely critical at Guadalcanal at that time. The gasoline situation was so desperate there at Henderson Field that they had resorted to this expedient of having the Vireo trying to run the gauntlet towing a barge load of aviation octane gas up there. They had assigned one destroyer up there, Meredith, to go with her. The destroyer suddenly wigwagged over--this was a few days before--a message to the Vireo, that there was a Japanese task force just over the horizon and for all hands to abandon the Vireo post haste and come aboard the destroyer, which they did. They cut loose their tow and all went over to the destroyer whereupon some Japanese aircraft hove in sight and promptly sank the destroyer with an extremely heavy loss of life and left the old Vireo floating around out there. She was floating around, and the idea was to get a pick-up crew aboard her and try and bring her back.

Q: And the gasoline was still intact?

Commander Melhorn: We never saw the gasoline. I was part of the pickup crew, and there was the old Vireo out there bobbing along like a cork, and we got her started and brought her down to Noumea. I went to see Admiral Turner just to say hello and thank him for bailing me out of Colhoun. He said, "What are you going to do?"

I said, "I'm here for assignment."

He said, "Well, they have some motor torpedo boat squadrons up there in Tulagi. They have an officer who just broke his leg, and they need a replacement. How would you like to go up there?"

I said, "Well, Admiral, that's all right with me. I don't know anything about PT boats, but I'll go." So I hung around Noumea until the next convoy was going up, and I went aboard President Jackson, I believe. We arrived at Lunga Point the morning of November 12th, and things were really heating up. Everybody knew that there was a Japanese battleship task force due in and that we were going to contest the passage. This was the morning before the great Battle of Guadalcanal with the San Francisco and this wild melee that they had up there. We were raided in Guadalcanal a couple of times--just routine raids that day--and then that evening I took my detail I had taken up with me back to Guadalcanal kicking and screaming, a couple hundred survivors of the Hornet. The Hornet had gone down at Santa Cruz, and while I was in Noumea all the Hornet survivors were out at a camp on the outskirts of town, and they all thought they were going back to the States.

Anybody who survived a ship down there figured they would go back to the States, but it hardly ever worked that way. I took orders to the survivor camp with a draft requisition for a couple hundred men who were needed in various capacities out there in Guadalcanal. So I had disembarked at Lunga Point with my men and was taking a part of them over to Tulagi--the motor mechs who were going over there to work with the PT boats, and we were all placed aboard the Bobolink, another old bird-class sweep and went chugging across the sound toward Tulagi that night. Of course, unbeknownst to us, on either side of us, we just missed this melee by about 30 minutes. On either side of us, closing at about 20 knots, were the two opposing forces, and we steamed right down the middle crosswise and got into Tulagi just in time to see all hell break loose out in the sound behind us.

Q: This was one of your lucky breaks again.

Commander Melhorn: It certainly was. And this was the night, of course, that they had this terrible melee out there which had been developed many times by historians. We saw the whole thing from the top of the hill.

Q: You actually could see it?

Commander Melhorn: Oh sure, you could see the whole thing

from the top of the hill in Tulagi. These flashes and tracers were going off all night long, and came the dawn and there was really an unforgettable sight out there, to look out towards Guadalcanal into this open water, and here were all these completely unrecognizable, blackened, smoking hulks.

Q: This is at night now?

Commander Melhorn: This was the next morning.

Q: But at night you could see the forms of the ships?

Commander Melhorn: No, you couldn't see the ships. All you could see were the tracers and the muzzle flashes, and the hits. But you didn't know who was getting hit. You just knew that there was a hell of a battle going on.

Q: Could you identify which side was which?

Commander Melhorn: Not a bit, because there was a melee out there. As Admiral Morison said in his volume five on the Guadalcanal campaign, they tried to reconstruct this, what went on from the ships' tracks, and all they could get, the best that could be said about it was that it was a melee.[*]

---

[*]Samuel Eliot Morison, The Struggle for Guadalcanal, Volume V of History of United States Naval Operations in World War II (Boston: Little Brown, 1949), pages 235-258.

The next morning one ship that was recognizable was the Aaron Ward, which had, I think, taken a hole in her condenser and lost steam and was lying out there dead in the water. Way over by Savo was a Japanese battleship, and she suddenly decided that she was going to take Aaron Ward under fire. So here came these great big battleship shell splashes close aboard, and at that point white smoke pouring out of Aaron Ward's funnels; she was preparing to take salt water into her boilers to get out of there. Anything you could get. So she came ripping into Tulagi harbor with Commodore Tobin aboard.* He had been with Dad on Admiral Richardson's staff.** He was the division commander for Aaron Ward's division.

Q: I'm sure at that point they didn't care what they were putting in their boilers if it would work.

Commander Melhorn: That's right. Portland was out there steaming around in circles with a jammed rudder, and that particular night, Atlanta was off in the distance with her back broken and she wasn't going anyplace, and the rest of the ships out there were just, as I say, masses of smoking molt.

Q: How did you feel? Weren't you just practically crushed to see--how was your emotional reaction to it?

---

*Captain Robert G. Tobin, USN, Commander Destroyer Squadron
**Shortly before the start of World War II, Melhorn's father was on the staff of Admiral James O. Richardson, Commander in Chief U.S. Fleet.

Commander Melhorn: I don't recall if I was particularly crushed by the thing. I knew we were all pretty excited when <u>Aaron Ward</u> was taken under fire, but we had things to do, and these things were all part of the game.

Q: You get on with it?

Commander Melhorn: You get on with it. <u>McFarland</u>, which was another World War I destroyer, had been hit by Japanese aircraft astern and had lost her rudder and had all kinds of steering problems. She had been lying up there in the back channel in Tulagi while they made a coconut log rudder for her and ran the thing off the after winch. Her skipper was sort of the harbor master and acting super there at Tulagi.

Q: You're probably one of the few people in history who got a balcony seat at the battle.

Commander Melhorn: Well, there were lots of people on Tulagi, and everybody was looking that night. We went down the following night, which was the night of November 13th, and the PT squadron to which I had just reported, this MTB Ron 3, was the only firepower that we had left there at the time, and another Japanese battleship task force was expected in that night.*

---

*MTB Ron 3--Motor Torpedo Boat Squadron Three.

Admiral Lee was around, Willis Lee, someplace with his battleships.* This would have been South Dakota and Washington. But they didn't know whether or not he was going to make it. The skipper of McFarland briefed us as to what we would do that night. The briefing amounted to: "There is a Japanese task force due in about midnight, and we may have a battleship task force due in about midnight. Go out and get the Japs." And that was the extent of the briefing. So about 10:00 o'clock, we pushed off.

Q: How many of you were in the squadron?

Commander Melhorn: I think we put out that night certainly no more than five boats, because the rest of them were down for mechanical, or they'd been hit. I know one of the first things I saw when I went to the PT base was this PT boat sitting up with its bow out of the water and the whole bow had been absolutely shredded, exposing the head. The toilet bowl was right up in the forepeak of the ship and all the plywood planking had been splintered and torn away, leaving this porcelain throne up there exposed for everybody. It apparently hadn't been touched but it really must have taken a shell hit right up forward.

Q: And the five of you were supposed to go out and stop the Japanese?

---

*Rear Admiral Willis A. Lee, Jr., USN, Commander Task Force 64.

Commander Melhorn: So the five of us were to go out and stop these Japs and be sure we didn't hit Admiral Lee. The only way that we could communicate with these task forces to establish recognition was to go through the minor war vessel challenge, which was a letter code by a flashing light we would have to do with an aldis lamp or a lamp gun. If anybody thought that we were going to be challenging the wrong group with a light they were out of their mind. If you challenge the wrong group, that's the end of you. So we went out there and it wasn't a successful sortie that night--some of our boats fired on a rock out there. One of our boats, and it might have been mine--I don't know--I was just an observer night--let four torpedoes go at Portland, which was still out there steaming around in circles, and promptly drew a cry of rage when all four missed and drew a blast from the Portland which thought that was pretty dirty pool. Then we came back and the Japanese task force did come in and did bombard Henderson Field and Lunga Point, and then withdrew.

The next night was the night of the battleship action when the Washington and the South Dakota did show up and we did have boats out. I was not out that night, but this was the night that Admiral Lee sent his famous message, "This is Ching Lee. You boys know who I am." The substance of the message was, "Stand clear, I'm coming through"--which they did. Then, of course, everyone knows what happened that night."[*]

---

[*]See Morison, The Struggle for Guadalcanal, Pages 270-287.

Q: Expand on that a little bit, however, to put it in its context.

Commander Melhorn: This was the culminating battle of the three-day engagement of the Battle of Guadalcanal, and left the sound still in our hands. By all odds it was the crucial sea battle of the Guadalcanal campaign, because the Japanese threw everything they had left at us, and we turned aside the attack.

Q: Left it still in our hands.

Commander Melhorn: Yes. Then from there on we just settled down to protect Guadalcanal--this was our job--and to interdict any Japanese forces that might be coming down. Our work was strictly at night. We never went out in the daytime, because we were fair game then for any hostile aircraft that might be in. So we would set up interdicting patrols the length of the coast of Guadalcanal from the Tassafaronga up past Savo, up past Cape Esperance, and down to Kokumbona and down to Coughlin Harbor. It was about this time that we began getting these "ultras" which were the code intercepts from Admiral Nimitz's headquarters to the effect that--well, one came in one night that said there was a Japanese submarine expected to surface off Lunga Point and gave the coordinates at such and such a time.* The message read, "There is a SOB aboard, X-ray, get him, X-ray." In other words there was some VIP coming in. So we sent a boat out under Jack Searles, who was there at the appointed time at the appointed place, and right on the dot this submarine surfaced right in front of him--probably heard the noise of the PT boats' engines and figured those were the engines of his own surface boat coming out from the Japanese-held coast there at Guadalcanal to make the transfer. So the Japanese submarine surfaced right in front of him, and Jack fired four torpedoes into him and that was the end of that, for which Jack got the Navy Cross and everybody else on the boat got the Silver Star.**

Q: Where did these messages come in? To the squadron headquarters?

Commander Melhorn: They would be relayed to the squadron headquarters. We had no way of copying messages down there. They would come in to somebody who was copying and would either come over from Guadalcanal or from the command there at Tulagi.

Q: Was this the beginning of the codebreaking which we were discussing at Pearl?

---

*Admiral Chester W. Nimitz, USN, Commander in Chief Pacific Fleet. Attached to his command at Pearl Harbor was a codebreaking unit which was decrypting Japanese radio messages and providing intelligence from those messages to operational forces.
**Lieutenant (junior grade) John M. Searles, USNR, of PT-59 sank the submarine I-3 with two torpedoes on the night of 9 December 1942. See Morison, page 319.

Charles Melhorn - 10

Commander Melhorn: Well, it certainly was not the beginning of it, but it was part of the continuing process.

Q: Your first experience with it, I should say.

Commander Melhorn: It was our first experience. The next big action was the battle of Tassafaronga, which I believe was on the 30th of November, 1942. We were set to go out that night. There was a very able Japanese admiral, Tanaka, who had been really a thorn in the side of the U.S. endeavor down there with his persistence and his skill in handling destroyers.* It developed after the war that he had spent a lot of time before the war training his ships in night tactics, and they were very good at it--particularly the night torpedo work. We were set to go out on this night, because we were always having brushes, little fire fights, with Tanaka's destroyers, and we were told very grandly that we could stay in that night, to stay out of the way, that "the first team" was arriving and would take care of these people. So we stayed in. About 2:00 o'clock in the morning we were ordered frantically out to go to the assistance of "the first team".

Q: What was "the first team"?

Commander Melhorn: Well, "the first team" was Admiral Wright's

---

*Rear Admiral Raizo Tanaka, IJN, Commander Destroyer Squadron Two.

cruiser squadron.* By the time we got out there, Northampton had sunk, Minneapolis had her bow blown clear to the number one turret and was dragging the bow, I believe, below it. New Orleans had her bow blown off past the number two turret, and Honolulu was nowhere to be seen. We spent the rest of the night trying to get survivors in and shepherd these stricken cruisers into Tulagi. What had happened was that Tanaka had come along and without firing hardly a shot had let go a spread of torpedoes and practically wiped out our cruiser line. I think we got one destroyer that night--our group got one Japanese destroyer that night--it was hardly a trade. The third ship to be very badly hit was Pensacola. She had taken a hit under her mainmast. I remember her coming into Tulagi Harbor and her mainmast was completely scorched, and they unloaded bodies off of her that almost filled up a tank lighter, and these corpses were all charred. It was just like taking cord wood off, for temporary burial over there in Tulagi.

The next real action was the night of December 12th. In the meantime, we had had another squadron come in, and one of the boat captains had been an old friend of mine from APD days. He had been riding McKean while I was in Colhoun. He didn't know the waters off Coughlin Harbor which was outside the sound down beyond Cape Esperance. His name was Frank Freeland.** I said, "Frank, I'll go along with you and show

---

*Rear Admiral Carleton H. Wright, USN, Commander Task Force 67, embarked in the USS Minneapolis.
**Lieutenant Frank Freeland, USNR, of PT-44.

you the water down there." So I jumped into the boat. I just went out as an observer that night, and we arrived on station on schedule. There was a possibility of an intercept that night. A Japanese submarine was expected in, and we were looking for him. About 12 o'clock, midnight, there were flashes behind us up between Savo and Cape Esperance, and it was apparent that a pretty good fight was making up there. Frank wanted to head right on in, but I suggested that we go in behind them and catch them coming out. If we did it Frank's way, it would have meant a high-speed approach.

Q: Could you make your choice? Could you change what you were to do and go back on your own?

Commander Melhorn: Well, what we had been sent to do was make this intercept on this submarine at such and such a time. They didn't know he was coming in. There was just a possibility that he was coming in. But the time had come and gone, so we were more or less on our own up there and our own boats were being engaged and it was up to us to provide support. There was no question about...

Q: You weren't changing the mission on your own?

Commander Melhorn: No, not at all. Whenever anybody got

in trouble up there, all hands converged. The problem to have gone right in, would have involved a high-speed approach, and the problem was that when you make a high-speed approach in a PT boat you throw up a very high rooster tail. The water had such a high phosphorus content down there that this rooster tail stuck out and you could see it for miles and miles, even at night, so nobody made a high-speed attack. It just wasn't done up there. This was strictly Robert Montgomery in the movies and They Were Expendable sort of thing. But we always idled in with the mufflers down and tried to get into a shooting position. Then when it came time to get out, then we opened the mufflers, then we cranked on the throttles and got out of there at high speed behind smoke. But for the attack phase the watchword was stealth. So we started in behind this action that was swirling on ahead of us up in the sound as this destroyer column tried to punch its way through to the area of Tassafaronga. We were right behind it, and we could see tracers going off in all directions up in front, which meant that they were out there chasing our boats someplace. If you can see the tracer on a shell, you've got a pretty good idea that the shell is not for you because the tracer burns in the rear end of the shell. So we went on in.

Q: You were behind the attacking force?

Commander Melhorn: We were behind the attacking force. We

were practically the last ship in the attacking force, but we were waiting until they would make their move to come out to present a broadside to us, and we would be in a good firing position. We were not in a good firing position at the time, because we would have been a stern chase for the torpedoes. So sure enough, finally they began to turn, and we picked this up with the glasses. The quartermaster, as I recall, told Frank, "Captain, your target is on the starboard bow." And we could see this destroyer making a turn to the right up there which would present us with a good shot. We had passed, at this time, a destroyer which had been hit by one of our boats--we actually saw the hit. It was not a burning hit, it was just this great geyser of water that went way up above the mast on this hit, but all very, very silent. We didn't hear a thing. Of course our engines were making a noise, too, which is one of the reasons we didn't hear anything. Then the destroyer fell out of column. It later developed, it was the Teruzuki, which was a brand-new Japanese class of destroyer. We passed her, steamed on by. She was on our starboard hand as we went by. We passed her to pick up the rest of the action, so she was then well astern of us when we made out this first destroyer on our starboard hand crossing from left to right. At the same time I was standing behind the cockpit. There was an arrangement on these particular boats where you had the cockpit, and right behind the cockpit there were two .50-caliber machine guns in scarf ring mounts, side by side. I was standing up with my back resting against the gun mount acting as a lookout, and over on the port side I saw more destroyers suddenly coming in. I said to Frank, "Frank, I think we ought to shift target outboard. Otherwise we're going to be boxed." It was the apparent thing to do. As soon as he saw them, I never would have had to tell him. He was the boat captain, anyway. So we shifted targets. Then suddenly we saw two more even further on our port hand, which meant we were really in a box then, because we were surrounded then on an arc from beam to beam ahead with hostile ships. Just at that moment, the Teruzuki burst into flame astern which made us a complete silhouette, like daylight, and the shells started coming in. So we turned--we had to abort the attack--and turned and started out on high speed. The shelling was extremely heavy. So much so that I can still smell the cordite. The whole air around there was nothing but splashes and cordite. We finally got out of there without a hit, for some reason, and went out under the lee of Savo, and turned again to make another attack. We figured we had gotten clear and they would have to be coming out of there sooner or later. We'd slowed and we were starting in, and just then I saw behind this burning destroyer a muzzle flash and no tracer. Well, when I didn't see the tracer, I figured "that's for us." So I jumped down into the cockpit for some reason or other, and I was no sooner in the cockpit than we took a direct hit abaft the .50-caliber scarf ring mounts. This completely wiped out the whole rear end of the PT boat. I can remember looking back to see what was left back there, and it was just a black outline of the hulk with little tongues of flame around a void of what used to be the engines. Having been a battery officer on a destroyer myself, I could just hear that Jap gunnery officer over there knowing that he had his hit, saying, "No change, no change, shift to rapid fire." I knew that things were going to get pretty sticky around there pretty quick. There were figures running toward the bow. Frank Freeland started aft, and he muttered as he went by me something about going to the life raft.

Someone on the bow hollered, "Shall we abandon ship?"

And he said, "Yes." He continued to go aft. I was just standing up there deciding that it was time to go. There were about five of us standing up there in various positions and we hit the water at once. As soon as he said go--we went. I had no sooner hit the water--I dove deep because I just had a feeling something was coming fast--and just about then another salvo hit and hit the tanks. We had torpedoes, depth charges, 2,700 gallons of high-octane gas, because we had expended practically no gasoline--there were maybe 2,000 gallons by then. The whole thing went up together. I was underwater a few yards away--no more than that--and it just paralyzed me. I was wearing a kapok jacket and the jacket took charge and pulled me up to the surface. I came up in a sea of fire. I couldn't move and I figured I was just going to burn to death here, and then suddenly another shell hit and threw up a tremendous splash. The splash came down all around me and put out some of the fire.*

Q: Freeland went down with the second...

Commander Melhorn: I never saw Frank again, but nobody on that boat would have survived. The biggest piece of the boat was about as big as my finger. It just blew the boat completely apart. There were people in the water. I saw one helmet and I heard some cries from in the flames. These guys were out of it--they were gone.

Q: You were the only one of the crew...

Commander Melhorn: I was the only one I could see. So remembering what had happened to Little and Gregory, which had been sunk before out there, and then the Japanese ships came around and ran through the area and ground up everybody they could with the screws. So I figured that we were possibly going to be in for the same sort of thing. So I hollered

---

*For a longer description of the same action, also quoted from Melhorn, see Robert J. Bulkley, Jr., At Close Quarters: PT Boats in the United States Navy (Washington: U.S. Government Printing Office, 1962), pages 97-99.

Charles Melhorn - 11

for anybody that happened to be there. I didn't know anybody was there, but I said, "Get clear of these flames." I was beginning to get some sensation back in my hands, and I began to swim very feebly to put as much distance as I could between myself and the flames. I never heard a thing from anyone.

Q: How many did it carry?

Commander Melhorn: We were 11 when we went out, and as far as I knew I was the only one left. So I got clear, and thought there's no use in staying out here; I'd better start swimming, and I knew that Savo was somewhere to the north. I couldn't see anything, but Sirius was in the northern quadrant at that particular time of the night, and I swam for Sirius until I could make out the tops of the peaks of the Savo volcanic cone. Then it was just a question of endurance from then on in.

Q: You still had your jacket?

Commander Melhorn: I had my jacket and I just kept on swimming. About 4:00 o'clock in the morning I heard a PT boat go by. I wasn't thinking too clearly--I had been bleeding from the ears and the mouth, and I'd gotten an awful water hammer and I thought perhaps I was bleeding from the rectum, too. My insides didn't feel too good from the concussion when the boat blew up. I was deathly afraid of sharks, because the natives on Savo, for a long time, one of their old tribal customs had been to set the dead adrift, and they had these Mako sharks down there, and since the Guadalcanal campaign had started this became the happy hunting ground for every man-eating shark in the South Pacific and the place was teeming with them. It was another reason why I wanted to keep on swimming. About 4:00 o'clock in the morning this...

Q: Was it self-preservation that kept you going? How many hours were you in the water?

Commander Melhorn: I was in the water about eight hours all in all. This is all right as long as you have a kapok jacket, you just keep pushing on. It's not a question of staying afloat. I could have stayed afloat all right, but it was awfully hard to swim, to make anything with that kapok jacket because the darned thing--you roll like a barrel and you cannot do an overhand stroke. I was a strong swimmer. I used to life guard at the P.C. Club in Long Beach before the war, and there was never any question about my ability to swim for a long ways, but I just couldn't make any headway in that damned kapok jacket so I was using sidestroke, backstroke, and a lot of breaststroke, and a lot of dog paddle--any way to just keep going. I heard the noise, as I say, just before dawn of the PT boat engine. I wasn't thinking too clearly, and I heard them go by me and I hollered, "I am on your port hand." Well, I was on their starboard hand, and they turned to port to pick me up and in so doing they picked up Dowling, who was a fireman, the only other survivor of the boat, who had been behind me. He didn't know I was ahead, and I didn't know he was behind, but he was also swimming slowly. He was in a lot worse shape than I was, and it was a good thing that they picked him up, because he had just about had it.

I finally got ashore on Savo that morning swimming. I started out swimming due north and wound up swimming due west. I had been set a quarter of the way around the island by the current, so I guess I swam about four miles all in all from the point of sinking. When I got there the natives picked me up. Savo was a kind of no-man's-land. Anybody who was sunk out there and could swim usually went for Savo. There were Japs living on it, and we had our own people living on it from time to time--survivors. The natives were all on our side, missionary trained, and they came down and provided me with a bamboo pole, and by then one of the cruiser float planes flew by shortly after that, and I had my undershirt up on the pole sticking up from the beach. He spotted this right away and Stilly Taylor came in in the boat and in two or three hours they were out looking for us, and nosed in and came in and picked me up.* There on the fantail of the boat were some of the survivors of my boat, all dead, laying out there under canvas, and the sharks had been at them, so the place was--the sharks had been busy that night. I have no idea how I ever managed to negotiate that four miles bleeding without attracting sharks. It's just inconceivable to me that it could be done. That ended my use of PT boats. I spent the rest of the time running daytime guard mail runs to Lunga Point.

Q: When you were swimming, were you able to think anything or were you just practically unconscious?

Commander Melhorn: Oh no. I was just thinking about keeping on going. One thing that I do recall, I was aware of what was going on around me, I saw the dipper laying upside down, flat on the horizon. It was completely flat. This is something that you never see in the northern hemisphere.

Q: Did you want to add anything to the last incident, such as your thoughts approaching Savo?

Commander Melhorn: Just to complete the PT phase of this thing, we were based aboard the tender Jamestown, which was a converted yacht, which was stuck up under netting, heavily

---

*Lieutenant Henry S. Taylor, USNR, commanding PT-40.

camouflaged in the back channel on Florida Island. The living quarters in there were certainly subpar. We had a "hot bunk" arrangement in that somebody would get out and somebody else would get in, and as a result the place was never cleaned up, because every time one of the stewards would come in there someone would throw a shoe at him. The lights were never put on; the temperature never got below 95°, the humidity never got below 98%, and it was pretty generally an unsatisfactory thing. We stuck this out until Christmas, and Christmas Eve there had been a liquor ship that finally had run the gauntlet and gotten in from New Zealand and deposited the Christmas ration of grog for all hands over on Lunga Point. Well, of course the first thing that happened from our comrades in arms from over on the Guadalcanal side was that they promptly hijacked the Tulagi supply of liquor, so we didn't have any. We were pretty burned up about this, and we got ahold of the squadron physician who had some tins of straight grain alcohol. With that we were able to salvage some of these little individual bottles like you used to get on the train when you'd order a highball in the club car of the train and they'd bring out an individual two-ounce bottle. Well, we scrounged some of those out from someplace--they were rum, bourbon, scotch--it didn't make any difference--and pooled it all with the straight grain alcohol and them promoted some number 10 cans of grapefruit juice. Over on the beach the natives over there had been drinking sort of a coconut mash which had a mild narcotic effect, and we requisitioned some of that stuff and poured it all into a great big garbage can on the deck of the Jamestown and proceeded to mix all this stuff up, got some ice, and had a Christmas party.

Of course, the results were just awful. Everybody got sick, as sick as a dog, because nobody had had anything to drink for several months. They all managed to get sick down in this black hole of Calcutta that we were living in. I can remember one thing--the head was tile and they had never bothered to rip the tile out and here was one of our officers, Lem Skidmore who is now a high-powered attorney in the city of New York.[*] He was an ensign at the time, and Ensign Skidmore was lying on this dirty tile without a stitch of clothes on, passed out completely, slumbering peacefully with all this filth and mess around him. He was using for a pillow a dirty swab that had been used to clean the urinals. This was typical of what a shambles that place was down below decks. As a result, the next morning we sent a negotiating party ashore to negotiate with the local chief to see if we could buy his village. We bought the village, lock, stock and barrel, and the villagers moved up the hill a quarter of a mile or so and proceeded to build themselves a new village.

Q: That is really something.

---

[*]Ensign Lemuel Skidmore, Jr., USNR.

Commander Melhorn: So we took over this, and that was the way we got away from the Jamestown. And things began to pick up from there, because life was absolutely unlivable aboard that miserable tender.

Q: It sounds just unbearable. You spoke of Skidmore. Any other names in your squadron that are not prominent?

Commander Melhorn: No. Jack Kennedy, of course, didn't get out until later. He came into the New Georgia campaign, and most of us were home by then. Most of the boat captains in my squadron were Ivy Leaguers and are all good solid citizens in New York, but nobody of national prominence to my knowledge.

Q: So from there you went to other duty?

Commander Melhorn: Yes. After I had been wounded the...

Q: Did you go to the hospital?

Commander Melhorn: No, I didn't go to the hospital. I spent a couple of days in the sick bay on the Jamestown. What I had was an abdominal compression from this blast, and after I got back on my feet, they put me on light duty, and I ran the afternoon guard mail trips over to Guadalcanal. By then the air over Guadalcanal was fairly secure, and we could operate in the daylight. Two force surgeons from the South Pacific Force, both of whom were long-time associates of my father's, one of them Dr. Dearing, came up to look at Purvis Bay, at that time being surveyed as a major fleet anchorage.* They came up there looking for a hospital site and I guided them around. Of course, they took one look at me and I guess I didn't look up to par, and they had heard what happened to me, and they said, "You've had enough. We're going to send you home." That's how I got back to the States.

In the meantime, before I had gotten hurt, I'd been thinking about getting into aviation, if for no other reason than it was one way to get out of Guadalcanal. I had taken the physical, and by the time I got back to San Francisco my orders were waiting there for me to flight training. I reported to Grand Prairie [Texas] for the primary training in April of 1943. It was certainly a case of out of the frying pan into the fire, because on my second dual--this was nothing more than an indoctrination flight--my instructor proceeded to run me through a set of high-tension wires between Dallas and Fort Worth, and we crashed on a country road down there. The instructor crawled out, he had the controls at the time and simply was demonstrating to me how to land on a country road. It was strictly a bush league stunt. I guess he wanted to impress me or something.

---

*Captain Arthur H. Dearing, MC, USN.

Charles Melhorn - 11

Q: He did, I'm sure.

Commander Melhorn: He certainly did. He crawled out on the wing and said, "I know people who have been court-martialed for this."

And I said, "Well, I would imagine so." In the meantime other planes saw us down there on the road, so we knew that help was on the way.

Q: You weren't hurt?

Commander Melhorn: Neither of us were hurt. No. The plane was pretty badly bent out of shape. It was a two-bladed prop and it had taken half of each blade off as he went through the wires and we were trailing all of these high-tension wires down the highway where we had snapped them. We had completely severed them, and we had made no ground connection at the time so there was no fire.

Q: I observe that these things always happen to you when you're sort of along for the ride. Isn't that true? The PT boat, you were showing Freeland the ropes, and here you were almost an observer.

Commander Melhorn: I wasn't an observer; I was really a student.

Q: You didn't have control.

Commander Melhorn: No, I didn't have control, but I had every reason to be there. The instructor was quite shaken by this whole thing, because he saw his Navy career, he had just been commissioned himself, he had just gotten his wings and had been ploughed back into the training program. He saw his career snuffed out there at the spot, and we were talking about it, and finally it occurred to me that as long as he was in the airplane that I could not be held responsible for anything that happened. I asked him about that, and he said, "Yes, that's so."

So I said, "Why don't you tell them that I froze at the controls, then? That gets you off the hook, and they can't do anything to me as long as you're in the airplane." He chewed that around for a while and thought that was a pretty good idea, and maybe we could try it out. So sure enough, when we got back to Grand Prairie, that's the yarn that he presented to the chief flight instructor. The chief flight instructor didn't believe a word of it, but at least it got him off the hook, so this was accepted around.

Q: And he probably wasn't anxious to wash the guy out anyway.

Commander Melhorn: He wasn't anxious to wash him out, and

I figured they didn't bring me back 5,000 miles to wash me out in an A stage dual, so I was fairly sure that nothing was going to happen to me. I went through that Grand Prairie with the all-time record. Nobody every got--they wanted to get me out of there before I spilled the beans, before I changed my mind and my check pilots would come out with long gray beards, real Santa Claus figures, to just move me along. So I was down at Pensacola concluding my flight training almost before I knew it and got my wings in the fall of that year, and then went down to Jacksonville, ultimately to Miami for operational training in the Grumman TBF.

Q: And of course, you liked it?

Commander Melhorn: Well, the torpedo racket was something I knew something about.

Q: I mean you liked the flying?

Commander Melhorn: Flying was never a great job for me. If you fly properly you've got to work at it, and I used to work at it pretty hard.

Q: But I always thought that you would have to love it or like it particularly to be able to do it.

Commander Melhorn: I certainly liked the flight pay.

Q: But you weren't consumed with an overall passion or love of flying?

Commander Melhorn: No, I never was. I enjoyed flying, and I certainly enjoyed the challenge, particularly instrument flying. I know the type you mean. I've run into aviators like that where they've actually told me that they prefer flying to sex.

Q: Really? I've never heard that.

Commander Melhorn: Absolutely. I know of one officer who is high in naval aviation today--he's still on the active list--who told me just exactly that. But that was never my bag, and there was a real need for torpedo pilots, because nobody was volunteering for VT in those days. Everybody wanted to be a fighter pilot. That was where the glamour was, and the F4U and the F6F were just coming on the line. They were mightly good airplanes and everybody wanted to fly them. But my experience was in torpedoes, and I thought I could be of more use in a torpedo capacity.

Q: Did you have a choice?

Commander Melhorn: Well, you could put in for something. You could put in for these things. So I wound up in them and was at Miami for operational training and had a bad midair collision one afternoon out over the Gulf Stream off Miami. We had been out with a 15-plane formation, which I was tail-end Charlie, making bombing runs out there, and we were accomplishing the rendezvous through towering cumulus clouds which were sort of like pillars with the bases at about 3,000 feet. There was clear area between them, but the rendezvous was pretty difficult. We came on up and the plane ahead of me was staying on the outside arc, which meant that all he could use to rendezvous was a speed advantage. It meant that if he had stayed on that arc it would have taken him the rest of the afternoon to join up. So after watching him for some time, I cut inside of him, which was not good form, but it was obvious to me that if we were ever going to get rendezvoused I was going to have to cut inside of him, and I kept him in sight as I did so, and climbed on in on a chord across the arc which is the way to rendezvous. Suddenly he got the idea that he should come in on another chord and began to come in on my starboard quarter. I saw him, and he kept closing and closing, and closing, and it was obvious to me that he didn't see me. I could see him looking up again over his starboard bow, because he had the formation in sight out there, but he wasn't looking inside because he didn't think anybody was up there. Well, I was up there.

Finally, he went out of sight behind me and below me, and I thought, I'd better get out of here. So I pulled back on the stick and climbed on up to where my air speed fell off to the point where I had to level off. The moment I leveled off, I was struck from below by him. He had come up right under me the whole way and had never seen me, and we had this wild midair collision. His prop sliced through my engine right behind the prop and cut all the gas lines, and I turned into a comet right off the bat. He just fell away, and I was burning very, very bad, and it was apparent to me that we had to go--I had two crewmen in the back end. So I picked up the mike and said, "Let's go." Then I waited until my pants began to burn up. The fire was then coming through the fire wall, and my flight suit began to char, and I just opened up the starboard canopy and went out. I was tumbling in the air as I rolled off the end of the wing, and I was still rolling when I pulled the rip cord, the "D" ring. Because I was tumbling, the drogue chute, instead of streaming up my back as it normally did, came up between my legs and up in my face and held on my face. By the time I could get the thing clear, by then all the shroud lines came whistling up between my legs, and I was upside down when the chute opened and took charge. I did a half-gainer there that almost broke my back and just about knocked me out, and when I finally came to and looked around, there was only one chute which had blossomed close by. It was my radioman, and the plane by this time had gone on down and crashed in the water, and the radioman was hanging upside down in his harness and was hanging by one strap which was hung up on his ankle. Apparently what had happened was that he had been in the back with his chest strap unbuckled, just sitting there and all of a sudden we had this midair collision. He didn't figure he had time to buckle his chest strap because of the fire, so he just went out and, of course, with his chest strap unbuckled, he almost came out of it. We rode down together, and we were talking as we went down. We hit some turbulence and began to swing at about the 4,000-feet level, and he lost control there and fell, and fell 4,000 feet to the water, and that was the end of him. The gunner never did get out of the ball turret. It was hard to get out of anyway and there simply wasn't time for him to get out.

I went on down and slipped the chute and wound up in the water again, and thought, well, here we go again. So I started swimming for Baker's Haulover, which was some miles away at the north end of Miami Beach. After two or three hours, a Coast Guard boat came out and picked me up and took me on in. We looked for my radioman but from 4,000 feet, he had no chance, and I had drifted some distance away from him anyway.

Q: Did he realize that this was going to happen to him, or have you any way of knowing from your conversation?

Commander Melhorn: No, he was just trying to hang on until we hit that turbulence and he ran all the way down. He was running just as hard as he could. That was the end of that particular episode.

Q: At what point, then, did you complete your flight training?

Commander Melhorn: Well, I was in operational training at the time. We all went through flight training in grade, all these boys that had been pulled back out of the fleet. The idea was that we were senior to most everybody in the squadrons that we went to, and they thought it was unwise to send us out being senior in time of service but really junior in time of experience in the air, so they kept us as instructors for a while to build up our time. I finally reported to a torpedo squadron in the Pacific Northwest at Klamath Falls. I went in as the number two man and had only been there a month before the skipper augered himself into Clear Lake which we were using for a bombing target. So that left me as the skipper of the squadron. I was acting for some time and finally got orders as the permanent skipper, so I deployed with the squadron in the spring of 1945 and we joined Cowpens, a CVL, with the

Third Fleet just in time to make Halsey's last assault against Japan.

Q: When you say augured, do you mean screwed himself into the ground?

Commander Melhorn: What it was was a target fixation. I mean augured in the sense that he practically screwed himself into the lake, in that when you're in a dive, to stay on target you frequently revolve about the axis of the dive. This is just part of the mechanics of the dive. Hence, augured himself right into the lake, because it just came up on him so fast, he didn't even know it.

As to the strikes against Japan, the highlights of those strikes were the final assaults against the Japanese fleet, which lay behind its guns and the guns of its protective shore batteries in the Inland Sea. My target on the 24th day of July was the heavy cruiser Tone, which we did not hit. We gave it several near-misses. Then four days later we went in and my target on this occasion was the Haruna--the same ship for which Colin Kelly and the B-17s had been given the Medal of Honor for sinking in the early stages of the war off the Philippines, but the Haruna had been very much in the war ever since.* And there she was still shooting on the

---

*Captain Colin P. Kelly, Jr., USA, attacked a Japanese warship on 10 December 1941, subsequently determined to be the cruiser Ashigara. Kelly was killed in the course of returning from the mission. Calling the ship he attacked Haruna was a case of mistaken identity.

28th of July 1945. As soon as I found out what our target was, and remembering that we had not done very well against the Tone, I told my people, "We're going in here, and we're going to be against all this flak again, let's make damn sure we get this ship. If we don't, they're going to send us back in this afternoon." So we really did a job on the ship. We were carrying general purpose bombs, a circumstance over which we had no control, so that all we did was clean off the topside. You don't sink battleships with general purpose bombs, but we certainly put her out of action at least as an antiaircraft platform. I lost one pilot on that strike; it was the only loss I had in the squadron for the war.

We were ranging up and down Honshu and Hokkaido and hitting airfields preparing to knock out Japanese air power in preparation for the Kyushu landings which were coming up. Then suddenly the atomic bomb was dropped, and it was announced throughout the fleet, and I felt, as did many other pilots, obsolete from that moment on.

Q: I think that's interesting, your comment about feeling obsolete when the bomb was dropped.

Commander Melhorn: I think we all felt that way. We certainly didn't have any taste for our final target which was the Tokyo Shibura Electronics Works—not the whole works, it was just

the power station which was one corner of the works. The
only problem was that this electronics works was in downtown
Tokyo practically, and when you put the flak circle overlays
on the Tokyo area, you could scarcely see the target area
for all the flak circles. We didn't know how many bombs they
had. We didn't know at the time the United States only had
two. We thought, what are we doing going in here when they
could really wipe this thing out with one of these new weapons
with no expenditure of life?

Q: I'm sure it would make a real depressant on your enthusiasm.

Commander Melhorn: Yes. We all knew the war was going to
be over. It was like, I'm sure they felt in World War I,
those soldiers in the Argonne on November 10 who were ordered
into action knowing the armistice was coming any minute.
If anybody got killed it was futile. The fact of the bomb
was announced throughout the Third Fleet right after the drop.
We had been given seven cities that we were not to attack--
that we were to stay away from--but no reason had been given
for that. Among the seven cities had been Hiroshima. Then,
of course, the morning of the announcement it was quite obvious
as to why we had been told to stay away from those seven cities,
that they were the seven cities, one of which had been ticketed
for destruction. When the war was over, Halsey had always

had a soft spot in his heart for Cowpens--I think that either his wife or his daughter had christened the ship.* So he was taking Missouri into Sagami Wan and needed sort of a courier carrier along with him, so he detached Cowpens from the Third Fleet, and we were the single carrier to go on in with him. There were other service ships, but we were the only carrier. The rest of the Third Fleet, of course, stayed deployed in full battle array off the coast.

Q: What date was that?

Commander Melhorn: It was after the Nagasaki drop--I would say this would have been about the 18th of August 1945. I think the 15th was the day they caved in. We got in there and were steaming around Sagami Wan, and all of a sudden a boat came in from Missouri with two of Halsey's staff officers to go in and arrange for the prisoner of war exchange--one of them being Harold Stassen.** At that particular time Stassen was a stalwart in the Republican Party, and there was good odds that he was going to be the next President of the United States, because his star was very high. I flew him in to Atsugi to arrange for this POW exchange, and the Army, the 11th Airborne Division, was just landing at this time from the Philippines. There was a little bitter taste in my mouth

---
*His daughter, Margaret Halsey Spruance, served as sponsor when the ship was launched and christened on 17 January 1943.
**Captain Harold E. Stassen, USNR, who had previously been Governor of Minnesota and later sought the presidential nomination on a number of occasions.

to hear this, "The war is over, so now let's start fighting each other again." The first thing that happened to me when I landed was that I blew a tire, and as I'm limping along the runway with Stassen in the back end, the Army bird colonel comes charging out on the taxiway waving this .45 and motioning me to take off--to get out. Obviously I had no business there, that this was an Army show, that the Army was now going to take over, and I thought, well, this is where I came in back in 1940. But I kept motioning to the rear end of my plane that I had business back there, and I stopped and Stassen got out, and this Army officer did the double-take of all times when he saw who my passenger was, and became deferential, and Stassen went off about his business. Then I flew him back to the ship that afternoon after I had a new tire flown in.

We had POW camps scattered all over Honshu there, and Stassen was being flown about in aircraft of my squadron. He took one trip to Niigata and then decided that he would come back all by himself on the Japanese train. There were no Westerners over there at all, and I doubt the Japs had the idea the war was over. He was absolutely fearless. He got on that train and came back to Tokyo all by himself. The day that I took him into Atsugi, when I walked over with him to a little striped tent over there that Japanese officials were waiting to greet our high officers to talk about these terms and arrangements, there was lemonade and so forth in there, everyone was anxious to be friends, I guess, and Stassen walked up to this Army general and said, "I have come to make such and such arrangements with regard to prisoner of war exchange, and I want you to do this and this, and this."

Whereupon the general said, "I have no authority to do this."

Stassen tapped him right on the chest and said, "Buster, you have no authority, period." Which laid it right on the line. He didn't hesitate to throw his weight around and, as I say, he was absolutely fearless.

Q: What was the distance he went on the train?

Commander Melhorn: Well, it was all the way from Niigata, which was on the Sea of Japan, way over on the western coast, all the way back to Tokyo, which involved a trip all the way across the spine of Honshu.

Q: Did you see the surrender ceremony?

Commander Melhorn: No.

Q: Were you in the flyover that happened that day?

Commander Melhorn: No, I was not in that flyover, but on

the first one--the big one. We put on an air show in which all the carriers in the Third Fleet participated; this was even before we had been detached to come in to Sagami Wan. Right after the war Halsey put everything up in the air, everything that would fly. And then we did a parade the length of the fleet. This formation was so big, it took us 50 miles to get it turned around so we could start off in the other direction. Being a minor commander of a minor squadron, I was way in the back of the pack, and the turbulence back there was enough so you could hardly stay in the air. As far as the eye could see ahead, there were nothing but airplanes--in this long, long column.

Q: It must have been spectacular.

Commander Melhorn: It was a spectacular show, it really was. We went into Tokyo Bay with Missouri to arrange for the surrender and being at anchor, we weren't in a position to launch aircraft in Cowpens so that particular flyover which was much smaller dimension, we didn't get to participate in.

Q: Did you have any personal contact with Halsey?

Commander Melhorn: No, none at all.

Q: He was much loved by the fleet according to repute, or

is that your experience?

Commander Melhorn: Yes. It has been charged in recent years, particularly in Clark Reynold's book on the fast carriers that Admiral Halsey was an embarrassment to the fleet in the later stages of the war.* But if that was so, I imagine this would be based on the performance in the typhoon.

Q: Philippine Sea?

Commander Melhorn: Well, when they lost the destroyers in the typhoon. If that was so, the word certainly never filtered down to any of us who were actually doing the fighting.

Q: It wasn't such an embarrassment that they didn't leave him in charge of the Third Fleet either.

Commander Melhorn: The man that we all loved out there, at least in my bailiwick, was Admiral McCain. I know that Admiral Mitscher seems to have the verdict of history right now, but Admiral McCain had our complete confidence.**

Q: You thought he was an excellent flyer?

---

*Clark G. Reynolds, The Fast Carriers: The Forging of an Air Navy (McGraw-Hill, 1968).
**Vice Admiral Marc A. Mitscher, USN, and Vice Admiral John S. McCain, USN, alternated as commander of the fast carrier task force.

Charles Melhorn - 13

Commander Melhorn: He was an excellent commander from the aviators' standpoint.

Q: You received some decorations and maybe you're too modest to mention them, but tell me what they were.

Commander Melhorn: I got the Navy Cross along with half the Third Fleet, I think, for the bombing runs on the 28th day of July--they were giving them out like popcorn.

Q: The flak was like popcorn, too, wasn't it, that you were flying through?

Commander Melhorn: Yes, but when I consider the awards program as it was in 1945, the Navy awards policy, against the Navy awards policy in 1942, at the time of Coral Sea and Midway, we were getting decorated in 1945 for things that they wouldn't even have gotten a pat on the back for in 1942.

Q: Then where did you go after the war, because you certainly didn't stop your Navy life at that point?

Commander Melhorn: We were putting the new carrier Leyte in commission and I went aboard her in the commissioning detail as flight deck officer. Then I had more-or-less routine duties on up the line, including one memorable tour as Jocko Clark's flag secretary, ComCarDiv Four in the Mediterranean in 1949 and 1950.*

Q: You have some stories to tell about that. I hope you'll tell them to me.

Commander Melhorn: Well, they broke the mold, of course, as everyone knows, when Admiral Clark retired; he is one of a kind. He had a not too satisfactory cruise over in the Mediterranean. In the first place, the fleet commander was Forrest Sherman.** I was led to believe there had been bad blood betwen Admiral Clark and Admiral Sherman going all the way back to their Naval Academy days when Admiral Clark had been involved in pouring ink down a plebe's nose and had been set back a year as a result, while Admiral Sherman who was his classmate, and had had some connection with this event, then became a year senior to him. There was no love between them at all. I know that on the second Med cruise in 1950, Tommy Moorer, now Chief of Naval Operations, was a staff operations officer, a very smooth, capable operator.***

---

*Rear Admiral Joseph J. Clark, USN, an aggressive officer who was one of the top fast carrier task group commanders during World War II.
**Vice Admiral Forrest P. Sherman, USN, Commander Sixth Task Fleet. Later, he was Chief of Naval Operations from 1949 until his death in 1951.
***Commander Thomas H. Moorer, USN, CNO from 1967 to 1970.

This is just an example of the relationship between Admiral Sherman and Admiral Clark. On our cruise in 1949, Admiral Sherman is the fleet commander, Admiral Clark is the carrier division commander. We're steaming downwind in Philippine Sea; we have one plane on deck; we're heading downwind; we're supposed to have a ready deck; this one plane is in the arresting gear. So we get this wigwag over from the flagship. "You are supposed to have a ready deck."

Back we go, "Affirmative."

"What is that plane doing on the deck? How can you have a ready deck when you have a plane sitting in the middle of the arresting gear?" Well, by the time we had turned into the wind, or anywhere into the wind line, we could have gotten rid of that plane, and ten more like it. It was just a question of putting a tractor on it and taking it out of there. We had a ready deck, but it was this small sort of bickering...

Q: An opportunity to dig.

Commander Melhorn: It was an opportunity to dig, and Admiral Sherman never, never lost an opportunity to take it out on Admiral Clark. There was also an incident involving Sherman's relief, who was Admiral Ballentine.[*] Admiral Clark had had a marriage of convenience with a young officer by the name of Herman Spencer Rosenblatt. Herman Spencer Rosenblatt had been an ACI officer, aircraft combat intelligence officer,

---

[*] Vice Admiral John J. Ballentine, USN, Commander Sixth Fleet

of a squadron in North Africa at the time Admiral Clark was skipper of one of the tanker carriers, the Suwannee, which participated in the North African landings of 1942. Admiral Clark, because of his stomach problems--he had half of his stomach operated out for ulcers during the Amelia Earhart search when he was in the Lexington back in the Thirties. It was questionable as to how far Admiral Clark was going to go on the promotion list because of his physical condition, but he met Herman Spencer Rosenblatt over there on the beach during the North African landings, and it's my evaluation that the two of them saw that each could be useful to the other. Herman Spencer Rosenblatt was the nephew of Judge Sam Rosenman, who was FDR's principal speech writer! Young Rosenblatt had good connections with the Mrs. Roosevelt entourage in the White House. So Rosenblatt and Admiral Clark joined forces. In due time, Admiral Clark became skipper of the new fighting lady, the new Yorktown, which was christened by Mrs. Roosevelt, and that might be a coincidence--I don't think so. He kept Rosenblatt with him all the way through the war. Rosenblatt was his flag secretary when Admiral Clark was covering himself with glory out in the Central Pacific.

Q: He even speaks of him in his book.[*]

Commander Melhorn: Well, we were over in the Med in 1950

---

[*] J.J. Clark, Carrier Admiral (New York: David McKay Company, Inc., 1967).

on the French Riviera, and we get a letter from Rosenblatt, who by then is long out of the Navy and is a practicing attorney in New York, that he would like to come back for two weeks' active duty. Well, Admiral Clark said, "By all means, come on back and you'll just be my aide." So Rosenblatt flies over comercially and arrives in Cannes with an aiguillette around his arm. We go to a party, a reception over there, and Admiral Ballentine is there with his aides, his chief of staff, his flag secretary, his flag lieutenant, and Admiral Clark is there with not three, but four aides.

Q: It sounds so funny.

Commander Melhorn: There was hell to pay over that. They were always getting at each other. While we were there, Rosenblatt had been connected in some way with procuring Rita Hayworth's divorce so that she could then marry Aly Khan, and at this time she was married to the Aly Khan and there was a connection there. Admiral Clark and Mrs. Clark then met Rita and the Prince and there was a frequent exchange of visits between the ship and the Château l'Horizon at Juan les Pines where they were in residence. It was decided that as a result of all this entertainment that the admiral should have a big party on the ship for all these counts and countesses and dukes and duchesses and lords and ladies.

Q: We call them jet-setters now.

Commander Melhorn: Yes, it was all these swingers over there. I was not invited to the party. I was going to be what Al Capp would term the outside man at the skunk works at this thing. My job was to be at the landing and make sure that everybody got put in the proper boat. This took some doing because not only was the Aga Khan, the fat old gentleman, invited to the party with the then current Begum, but also his former wife, the Princess Andre of Khan was also invited. I was under orders that under no circumstances should the present incumbent and the former Mrs. Aga Khan be put in the same boat at the same time. So I was there to see that this didn't happen. In due time this cavalcade of Cadillacs roars up and out came the Aga and all of his bodyguards and people, and I loaded them into the barge and sent them off. A few minutes later, the Princess Andre came up, and she rated the captain's gig, and off she went in that. Then it was evening, and I suddenly ran out of boats, and after about 20 minutes with these guests arriving all the time wanting to go out to the ship--no boats. So I got on the walkie-talkie and asked the ship where the barge was, and where was the gig? And they said, "All hell's busted loose out here. You'd better come on out." So I grabbed one of the motor launches and went on out just in time to see all this rushing around on the flight deck. What had happened was that the Aga Khan had arrived at the foot of the accommodation ladder--the ship, of course, never anchors in close aboard--it's always anchored well out, about a mile out, there in Cannes, because it has too much draft to come in. So the Aga Khan was at the foot of the accommodation ladder, took one look at it, and said he just could not get up the ladder--which was true. He was too fat. He'd have had a stroke halfway up.

Q: He was wider than the ladder, wasn't he?

Commander Melhorn: He was awfully wide. We had researched this thing very, very carefully, and it had been put to us that he was in excellent physical shape, that he played golf every day. What we didn't know, that he did play golf every day--he played one hole. So here he was out there in the boat. In the meantime, Rita Hayworth and the Aly Khan--the Aly Khan had just busted his leg up in Switzerland in a skiing accident and he was in a hip length cast, so he was going to have some trouble too, getting up this accommodation ladder, and there was this council of war going on between Admiral Clark and Captain Beakley at the head of the ladder on the quarterdeck how to get them in.* Some boatswain's mate came up with the idea that they would use the big airplane crane and take the whole shooting match up on the flight deck.

---

*Captain Wallace M. Beakley, USN, commanding officer of the USS Midway, which was Clark's flagship.

So they rigged the hoisting slings in the barge, and Admiral Clark went down to lend a little air of confidence to the proceedings. He got into the barge and they manned the boat crane on the flight deck and dropped the hook, and hooked on, and hoisted the boat with the Aga Khan, the Begum, the Aly Khan, Rita Hayworth, Admiral Clark, everybody got up to the flight deck, and were put inside this boat cradle on the flight deck. The only trouble with that was it left them 20 feet above the flight deck.

Q: Anyway they couldn't step down.

Commander Melhorn: They couldn't step down. Now came the problem as to how to get them out of the boat, because in the meantime the tomato juice was being served in silver goblets on the hangar deck, and there was some question as to how we were going to get the Aga Khan out of the boat on the flight deck down to the hangar deck. Some other genius then came up with the idea--we had these forklifts, so they got this forklift and they put a pallet on the thing, and they put a boatswain's chair on top of that with two people to hold the boatswain's chair, and they two-blocked the pallet on the forklift which just reached up to the deck level of the boat which was in the dolly. The Aga Khan simply stepped over the gunwale onto the boatswain's chair and sat down and

Charles Melhorn - 14

was lowered onto the flight deck level and then was trundled the length of the flight deck to the number one elevator. They manned the elevator, dropped the whole elevator with the Aga Khan sitting on the forklift which put him right at the tomato juice.

Q: It's awfully funny in knowing it, but I'm sure it wasn't funny at the time.

Commander Melhorn: Then, of course, the whole process had to be reversed to get him back off the ship.

Q: And it had to be done for every person in the barge.

Commander Melhorn: It had to be done for everyone else in the barge too. But that was no problem. At least they could walk the length of the flight deck.

Q: They were all a little bit agile, I presume.

Commander Melhorn: Rosenblatt, of course, was always a party to this sort of thing. This whole association--the fact that Admiral Clark became a confidant of the Aga Khan's and was consorting with movie stars--none of this stuff rubbed off well at all with Admiral Ballentine. So the cruise was not successful for Admiral Clark. He had his problems.

Q: But he did have the facility for doing the dramatic with a flair. Always with himself at the center.

Commander Melhorn: That's true. He appreciated a good press.

Q: Any other stories in the Med?

Commander Melhorn: One later cruise, I had gone from ComCarDiv Four through some usual rotations, and then went back to the fleet in VC-12, which was based out at Quonset Point, which was an airborne, early-warning, all-weather squadron. I realized that this was probably my last tour. I was beginning to get on in years, and I realized that this was my last shot at a flying billet in the fleet. Although I was part of the palace guard there at Quonset with little prospect of going to sea, I prevailed upon the skipper to let me take a team out. In 1955, in August, we boarded Ticonderoga. The air group was Air Group Three out of Jacksonville and we deployed from Mayport for the Med. Andrew McB. Jackson was the skipper of the ship. From my standpoint, as one of the minor commanders in the thing, it was not a very successful cruise. In the first place, we had a terrible fatality rate.

Q: The pilots?

Commander Melhorn: Pilots, the ship's force--one night off the coast of France, a Banshee came in, it was part of the all-weather Banshee squadron, jumped over the barriers and lit right in the middle of the catapult crew, took several people over the side--we lost several men on that.* There were numerous launching accidents, numerous landing accidents, some of which were fatal. It was an unlucky cruise, just almost ill-starred. None of these things, of course, were done deliberately, but it was just a bad show.

Q: Who was the skipper?

Commander Melhorn: A. McB. Jackson. It didn't hurt him at all. He's now a vice admiral. When you're on a ship and you go to assess it when it's all over, of course there are good times and bad times. I've always looked at it either the cruise was a plus or the cruise was a minus, and this cruise was a minus. There's just no other way to look at it. I had my own problems over there. I was making an instrument letdown to the ship one night and, as usual, it was as black as ink out there, and we were half VFR.** They would never let us practice the instrument approach equipment on the ship. There was never any time to practice it, and the ship would not make time to practice it, so that when we went out there

---

*Banshee--a McDonnell-built F2H fighter plane.
**VFR--visual flight rules (as opposed to instruments).

to do it, we were doing it for real. This has its drawbacks.

Q: Was that the skipper's fault?

Commander Melhorn: Well, Captain Jackson would have to have some responsibility for it. But anyway the timing interval in night instrument landing on a carrier is a pretty exquisite thing. It's something that takes practice. I know one night off Valencia my splinter group was landing, and we made our letdown and were coming in--we were half contact, half instruments. This is a miserable situation for a pilot to be in--when you're on your instruments and you have to look up to see if someone's ahead of you and so forth to try and keep your intervals straight. In the process I lost my scan. It was certainly pilot error. I have no intention to lay the blame for this on anyone else. I landed two and a half miles short in the water. I had two people with me and we were all picked up. We were a little cold, but we didn't flip over, although I had my wheels down at the time.

Q: Did you go under the water?

Commander Melhorn: Well, of course, the plane ultimately sank and we were lying out there in rubber life rafts and were ultimately picked up by a destroyer.

Q: But the plane didn't take you down with it?

Commander Melhorn: No. But these sort of things were always happening on the cruise. If they didn't happen to my unit, they were happening to some other unit, not only with the air group but with the ship's company. We went in to Beirut [Lebanon] and made the usual Mediterranean moor there to two great big mooring buoys, which were, in this particular case, fairly close to the mole of the outer harbor. We were there for three or four days and for some strange reason, I was on board one night and all of my people were also aboard, and all of a sudden the word was passed in the middle of the night, "Man the special sea details." I nudged my roommate, who was my airborne controller and always flew with me, and I said, "I wonder what that's for?"

He said, "I have no idea."

About two minutes later, again came over the 1MC, "Now man the special sea detail on the double. This is an emergency."

I was in the lower bunk and I kicked my roommate in the upper bunk and said, "Let's roll out of here right now. You get up and get the rest of the pilots and tell them to man their airplane and I'll see what's going on up there." I went up to the navigating bridge, and the navigator and the exec were there peering over this chart with big drops of sweat coming down off their foreheads. What had happened was that the ship had chafed clear through a great big mooring hawser, a great big wire hawser which had been chafing under the counter as the ship swung back and forth in the wind. The stern had swung free, and we were in the grip of a wind and were bearing down on a tanker which was full of aviation gasoline, which had a destroyer moored outboard of her. It was obvious that they could heave around on the anchor chain but that's all they could do. There was no steam--they were on a cold iron watch down in the engine room, and there was not sufficient steam to get the wheels turning at all. I just happened to have my planes spotted in the so-called pinwheel formation and were so positioned so they could exert a maximum amount of force.* I said to the navigator up there, "I'm all spotted for a pinwheel, can I give you a pinwheel here?"

And he said, "My God, yes. Right away." So I went running back to the fantail, and my pilots by then had manned their airplanes in their skivvies and were sitting there, and I gave a two finger, which is a full power turn up. They all objected to that because you don't rev up a cold engine--you warm it up, you don't go right to full power. But we went right up to full power on these things. I had three planes back there, three of my four planes, and we stopped that ship before it hit the mole, but not, however, before it had completely wiped clean the after gun house of the destroyer which was moored outboard the aviation gasoline, the white tanker.

---

*The planes in Commander Melhorn's squadron were AD-5Ws, propeller-driven Skyraiders equipped with radar for airborne early warning duty.

Charles Melhorn - 14

Q: Explain a little bit more to me now, what kind of wind were you making?

Commander Melhorn: The wind was blowing so that it was setting the stern of the ship down toward the mole.

Q: What did your planes do?

Commander Melhorn: I was able to stop that movement.

Q: You did it in the opposite direction?

Commander Melhorn: That's right. My planes were so positioned. They just happened to be there. The stern was swinging. The pivot was on the bow. The bow was still moored. The stern was swinging free and I was able to stop that motion.

Q: The thrust from your planes was sufficient going into the wind to just stop the ship swinging any further.

Commander Melhorn: That's right.

Q: And did you know it would do that?

Commander Melhorn: Well, yes. A pinwheel is a standard maneuver from a pinwheel spot. It's a standard way for a carrier to maneuver in a restricted space.

Q: That is used to maneuver?

Commander Melhorn: Yes. It's been used for years.

Q: But no one thought of it but you at that time?

Commander Melhorn: Well, things were pretty confused up there. Only the stern was spotted pinwheel. The bow had not been spotted. That was where we needed it, and I just happened to mention it in passing to the navigator and the exec that this was a possibility that might help some and it worked. As a result, I had to have three engine changes because the engines were ruined. There was practically molten metal dripping out of the exhaust stacks because we had to stay up at full power until the ship was able to make steam.

Q: How long was this?

Commander Melhorn: It was over an hour. We had the cowl flaps open all the way but, of course, there was no ram air circulating through the engine and the cylinder head temperatures were just out of sight. The oil pressure had dropped down to about zero.

Q: Well, you accomplished the purpose.

Commander Melhorn: It was a lot cheaper to replace three aircraft engines than to tow that aircraft carrier all the way from Lebanon to Gibraltar, which was the nearest dry dock that could have accommodated it.

Q: And the other two ships. It probably would have started a fire on the tanker.

Commander Melhorn: Yes. From then on my detachment could do no wrong. We had practically an open gangway. The captain would get mad and restrict the rest of the ship but we had the run of the beach. He figured he owed us one. He recognized it. Several of us got an unofficial letter for it.

But that was the last of the Med cruises. They finally got me back in the Pacific. I swore after 1945 I'd never go back into that big ocean, but I finally got on the staff of Admiral Brandley, ComCarDiv 15, which was an ASW group.* Then back to the North American Air Defense command at Colorado Springs. It was there that I had the coronary and I got retired back in 1961.

Q: So you fought the war from end to end and then some.

---

*Rear Admiral Frank A. Brandley, USN.

Charles Melhorn - 151

Commander Melhorn: There was nothing unique about that.

Q: Many people did it, but I think that your experiences are well worth recording and I found it completely absorbing. In 1961 you were retired--physical retirement. I think it's interesting to know what you've done now in your civilian pursuits.

Commander Melhorn: Well, the doctors suggested that I get into something quiet. I had a pretty bad jolt with this coronary and it was a couple of years before I could do anything.

Q: How long were you hospitalized?

Commander Melhorn: I was hospitalized three months, but convalescence was long and slow.

Q: Where were you?

Commander Melhorn: In the San Diego area. I finally went back to San Diego State and picked up a master's degree in history, and taught for a year there. Then it was apparent to me that master's degrees were a dime a dozen nowadays, and that no one can rely on them to be worth anything, so it looked like I was going to have to go for the Ph.D. So

Charles Melhorn - 15

I went on over to the new campus at the University of California at La Jolla and went into the Ph.D. program over there just in time--ironic, recommending the college life, university life, as something quiet--I got there just in time to hit the student revolt, particularly UCSD, which was under the fine Italian hand of Herbert Marcuse. The turmoil has been pretty heavy ever since.

Q: Were you involved with it?

Commander Melhorn: I was involved on the other end. I did what I could to check it without too much success. It wasn't all useless. I think some of us were able to make a mark in it.

Q: I would think so. But your--you have passed the orals and writtens for your Ph.D., and you are now in the process of writing your dissertation. What is the subject of your dissertation?

Commander Melhorn: Having written my master's degree thesis on the French default in the Rhineland in 1936, I thought I would now get into something that I knew something about, so I'm doing it on the rise of the aircraft carrier mostly in the period of the Twenties. The hypothesis in that is that some very astute heads in the Navy, notably Admiral Moffett, saw in the carrier, in the development of the carrier, a way around the strictures imposed on the U.S. Navy by the Washington Treaty. I think I'm going to be able to prove it.[*]

Q: I think you'll make a contribution. I really am touched by this interview. It's noteworthy, I think. You've made contributions, certainly, in your military life, and you are making a contribution in your civilian life. I'm sure that your dissertation will be a contribution to history.

---

[*]Commander Melhorn's dissertation was completed in 1973 with the title of Lever for Rearmament: The Rise of the Carrier. It was published in book form by the Naval Institute Press in 1974 as Two-Block Fox: The Rise of the Aircraft Carrier, 1911-1929.

Index to

Taped Interviews

with

Rear Admiral Kent C. Melhorn, MC, USN (Ret.)

and

Commander Charles M. Melhorn, USN (Ret.)

Aaron Ward, USS (DD-483)
    Sitting dead in the water from damage received during 13
    November 1942 Guadalcanal action, this destroyer took salt
    water into her boilers to beat a path to Tulagi when a Japanese
    battleship began to shell her, p. 96.

Accidents/Disasters
    Loss of U.S. destroyer Meredith (DD-434) in October 1942,
    p. 92; Melhorn is on board PT-44 as an observer when it is
    destroyed in December 1942, pp. 103-113; plane crash with
    instructor on dual flight during training at Grand Prairie,
    Texas, in 1943, pp. 119-120; midair collision off Florida
    in mid-1940s, pp. 122-124; Melhorn loses plane in Mediterranean
    during deployment on carrier Ticonderoga (CVA-14) in the
    mid-1950s, pp. 145-146; USS Ticonderoga breaks mooring lines
    at Beirut, Lebanon, and swings near gasoline tanker, saved
    by "pinwheel" maneuver, pp. 146-150.

AD-5W (Skyraiders)
    While on a Mediterranean deployment aboard USS Ticonderoga
    (CVA-14) in 1955 Melhorn ditches his plane during an attempt
    at a visual/instrument landing, pp. 144-146; Melhorn's quick
    thinking and the use of his squadron's planes in a pinwheel
    maneuver lessen the damage when the Ticonderoga breaks a
    mooring line near Beirut in 1955, pp. 146-150.

Aga Kahn III
    When this member of Indian royalty was invited by Admiral
    Joseph J. Clark to attend a party on USS Midway (CVB-41)
    in 1950, his physical condition dictated that extraordinary
    means be devised to get him aboard, pp. 139-142.

Aircraft carrier operations
    Melhorn's squadron aboard USS Cowpens (CVL-25) sees heavy
    action off the coast of Japan in 1945, pp. 126-128; Cowpens
    is only carrier at the site of the Japanese surrender in
    August of 1945, pp. 129, 132; carriers of Third Fleet participate
    in air show prior to surrender, p. 132; Melhorn's assessment
    of Halsey and McCain as carrier admirals, pp. 132-134; incident
    between VADM Sherman and RADM Clark concerning Clark flagship
    Philippine Sea's flight deck readiness in 1949, p. 136; party
    aboard Midway (CVB-41) with many celebrities hosted by Clark
    in 1950, pp. 138-142; accident-ridden Mediterranean cruise
    aboard Ticonderoga (CVA-14) in 1955, pp. 143-150; pinwheel
    maneuver employed aboard Ticonderoga in 1955 after mooring
    line breaks, pp. 146-150.

Alcohol
    When their share of Christmas grog from a New Zealand ship
    is intercepted by others in 1942, the crew of the gunboat
    USS Jamestown (PG-55) concocts a makeshift alcoholic punch
    that promptly incapacitates everyone, pp. 114-115.

Aly Kahn
> This member of Indian royalty and husband to actress Rita Hayworth was introduced to Admiral Joseph J. Clark by Clark's ex-aide Herman Rosenblatt and was invited with his family to a party aboard USS Midway (CVB-41) in 1950, pp. 138-142.

Army, U.S.
> Competition between Army and Navy medical departments to see who could reach air crash sites sooner at Rockwell Field, North Island, San Diego in 1914, p. 9; friction caused when a colonel from the 11th Airborne Division perceives Melhorn's arrival in Atsugi in August of 1945 as the Navy's attempt to steal glory from the Army's Japanese landing, pp. 129-130.

Atomic bomb
> Melhorn's feelings that as a torpedo plane pilot he was obsolete from the moment of the Hiroshima bombing in August of 1945, and his distaste that his squadron was sent on bombing missions endangering their lives at the bitter end of the war, when an atomic bomb could have been used, pp. 127-128.

Atrocities, World War II
> Colhoun (APD-2) crew members scavenge bodies of dead Japanese plane crew for souvenirs during Guadalcanal campaign in August 1942, p. 89; Japanese ships' use of propellers to ensure no survivors from U.S. ship sinkings, p. 109.

Awards
> Melhorn's World War II commendations, p. 134; degradation of medals from start of World War II to finish, p. 134.

Cannon, Joseph G.
> Influential, long-time member of Congress who helped arrange assignments for his friend, Medal of Honor winner Ernest C. Williams, p. 13.

Caribbean
> See: Dominican Republic, Haiti, Nicaragua

Carlson, Lieutenant Colonel Evans F., USMC
> As commander of the Second Marine Raider Battalion training in the San Diego area in 1942 displayed much evidence of his service in the Chinese army in the mid-1930s, especially concentration on guerilla tactics and political indoctrination, pp. 82-85.

Clark, Admiral Joseph J. "Jocko", USN (USNA, 1918)
> Animosity with Admiral Forrest Sherman and Sherman's successor as Sixth Fleet commander, Vice Admiral John Ballentine, pp. 135-136, 138, 142; value of relationship with politically connected aide Herman Rosenblatt, pp. 136-138; hosts party for jetsetters on board flagship Midway (CVB-41) in 1950,

Codebreaking, results of
    See: Intelligence

Colhoun, USS (APD-2)
    This high-speed transport, embarked with Marines, is sent
    to Martinique to intercept French carrier Bearn in 1941,
    pp. 81-82; commanding officer, LCDR George Madden, insists
    that his officers wear service whites regardless of task
    in mid-1942, pp. 86-88; crew members scavenge bodies of Japanese
    airmen they shot down in 1942, p. 89.

Coolidge, Grace G.
    Wife of President Calvin Coolidge who impressed Melhorn when
    they met in the mid-1920s with her thoughtfulness and grace,
    p. 32.

Counterintelligence
    See: Espionage

Cowpens, USS (CVL-25)
    Melhorn's torpedo plane squadron deploys aboard in Spring
    of 1945, pp. 125-126; chosen by Admiral Halsey to be the
    only carrier present at the signing of the Japanese surrender
    in August of 1945, pp. 129, 132.

Denver, USS (C-14)
    This cruiser patrols off the west coast of Nicaragua in the
    mid-1910s, p. 9; while anchored off Corinto, Nicaragua in
    mid-1910s crew is beaten at baseball by residents of Chinandega,
    pp. 7-9.

Disarmament
    See: World Disarmament Conference

Dixie, USS (screw steamer)
    After a cruise to the Caribbean in 1908-1909 this ship picks
    up Marines at Hampton Roads to attend inaugural parade for
    Taft in March 1909, p. 6.

Dominican Republic
    Fourth Marine Regiment, under Colonel Pendleton, enters Santo
    Domingo at the government's request in 1915, pp. 10-14.

Edson, Lieutenant Colonel Merritt A., USMC
    Commands 1st Marine Raider Battalion when it embarks in high-
    speed transports to patrol East Coast in 1941-1942, pp. 81-82.

Espionage
    A suspected Japanese spy in Long Beach is apprehended after
    a retired military officer reports suspicious actions to
    Melhorn, who is in charge of the medical dispensaries in
    the area in the late 1930s, pp. 61-62.

Flight training
    Melhorn's experiences in flight school at Grand Prairie, Texas in 1943, including a crash while on a dual fight, pp. 117-120; operational training with a torpedo plane squadron in Florida, including a midair collision in mid-1940s, pp. 120-125; organization of students by rank during World War II, p. 125.

Forrestal, James V.
    As undersecretary of the Navy during World War II initiates policy of having management engineers visit naval installation to critique for efficiency, p. 70.

Freeland, Lieutenant Frank, USNR
    As an old friend from previous duty, Melhorn accompanies the newly-arrived Freeland as an observer of a motor torpedo boat (PT) mission around Tassafaronga that ends in disaster in December of 1942, pp. 103-109.

French Navy
    French carrier Bearn in Martinique considered a threat to the opening of the Panama Canal in mid-1941 draws U.S. Marines to neutralize ship; they are recalled when diplomatic solution is reached, pp. 81-82.

Germany
    Planned to seize Haiti during upheaval following assassination of President Sam in 1915 in order to control waterways leading to the Panama Canal; this was foiled by arrival of U.S. Navy and Marine Corps in 1915, pp. 22-23; treatment of the Melhorns in 1932 despite diplomatic passports, pp. 52-53.

Gibson, Hugh S.
    As top-ranking U.S. delegate to the World Disarmament Conference in 1932, p. 46; temperate drinking habits inspire naming of cocktail that is plain water with an onion, p. 49.

Gregory, USS (APD-3)
    Melhorn's first ship duty after commissioning was on this high speed transport commanded by LCDR William Brown who later commanded the Missouri (BB-63) when it ran aground in January of 1950, p. 81.

Guadalcanal campaign (August to November 1942)
    1st Marine Raider Battalion embarked on high-speed transports (APDs) practice for assault on Fiji Islands in July 1942, pp. 85-86; success of Marine landings from Melhorn's APD squadron, pp. 86-88; action on board high-speed transport Colhoun (APD-2), pp. 88-90; buildup on Lunga Point on 12 November 1942 for major engagement the following day, pp. 93-94; on their way to Tulagi, Melhorn and his mechanics narrowly miss being caught between Japanese and American forces and are able to view fighting on 13 November 1942,

between American and Japanese battleships proves to be decisive battle for holding Guadalcanal, pp. 99-100; Battle of Tassafaronga, p. 102.

See also: Motor Torpedo Squadron Three.

Hague, Frank
Infamous mayor of Jersey City, New Jersey tries to offer the city hospital to the Navy for use during World War II, but is flatly turned down when he refuses access to pertinent maintenance and operating information, pp. 67-68.

Haiti
American doctors stationed in Haiti in the early 1920s under terms of Haitian-American Treaty, pp. 19, 22, 34; medical personnel in 1920, pp. 21-22; German interest in Haiti in 1914-1915, pp. 22-23; health conditions in the late 1920s, pp. 25-26; American advisors assist in government in mid-1910s, p. 24; Rockefeller Foundation funds improvements to medicine, nursing, and sanitation using naval personnel, pp. 34, 38; influence of Haitian racism on medical appointments in late 1920s, pp. 38-39; Haitian senator of Melhorns' acquaintance's meeting with President Abraham Lincoln during U.S. Civil War, pp. 40-41.

Halsey, Admiral William F., Jr., USN (USNA, 1904)
Melhorn's assessment of his personality as Commander Third Fleet in 1945, pp. 132-133.

Haruna, HIJMS
Japanese battleship mistakenly credited as a kill to Army flier Colin Kelly in 1941 but subsequently attacked by Melhorn's squadron in 1945, pp. 126-127.

Health problems
Epidemics of spinal meningitis, measles, and pneumonia at Norfolk Naval Base in late 1910s, pp. 15-16; severe outbreak of flu across United States necessitates recruiting coffin builders at Norfolk in late 1910s, pp. 16-17, 19; yeomanette sent to Melhorn in Norfolk as having mumps later diagnosed as pregnant, pp. 17-18; smallpox epidemic in Haiti in the early 1920s, pp. 25-26; flu epidemic in Europe in 1932, p. 47.

Hornet, USS (CV-8)
After her loss in the Battle of Santa Cruz in October of 1942, some of her survivors instead of being sent home were requisitioned to motor torpedo squadron duty under Melhorn on Guadalcanal in November, 1942, pp. 93-94.

Hospitals, naval
Naval Medical School; Washington, D.C., pp 2, 20, 31-33; Norfolk Naval Hospital, pp. 15-19; San Diego Naval Hospital,

pp.55-56; community hospital in Jersey City offered to Navy during World War II, but refused, pp. 67-68.

Influenza
Conditions at Norfolk Naval Hospital during outbreak of this illness that swept across the country in the late 1910s, pp. 16-17, 19.

Intelligence
Occupation forces on Guadalcanal receive messages from Admiral Nimitz's Pacific Fleet headquarters obtained from broken Japanese codes, including one message that enabled a PT boat from Melhorn's squadron to sink a Japanese sub in December of 1942, pp. 100-102.

Jackson, Captain Andrew McB., USN (USNA, 1930)
As commanding officer of the USS Ticonderoga (CVA-14) in the mid-1950s, Melhorn assigns Jackson some of the responsibility for the absence of instrument approach flight training in his squadron and their subsequent difficulties, pp. 144-145.

Jamestown, USS (PG-55)
Substandard living conditions aboard this converted yacht that housed the crew from Melhorn's PT squadron in 1942 eventually led to the crew's purchase of a village on Florida Island for improved habitability, pp. 113-116; Christmas party with makeshift alcohol aboard in 1942, pp. 114-115; Melhorn recuperates from PT sinking wounds in sickbay, p.116.

Japanese Operations
Spy in Long Beach, California apprehended after Melhorn passed along a report from a retired officer in late 1930s, pp. 58-59; sub patrolling the entrance to Pearl Harbor in the late 1930s, pp. 61-62. Strategy in the Guadalcanal landings in 1942, p. 87; survivors of downed plane refuse rescue and their bodies are later scavenged by U.S. transport crew member in August of 1942, p. 89; sink U.S. destroyer Meredith (DD-434) with heavy loss of life in October 1942, p. 92; battleship shells damaged destroyer Aaron Ward (DD-483) after fierce action at Guadalcanal, p. 96; submarine sunk off Lunga Point, due to precise intelligence received at Motor Torpedo Squadron 3 from Pacific Fleet headquarters in December, 1942, pp. 101-101; RADM Raizo Tanaka, IJN wreaks havoc on U.S. cruisers during Battle of Tassafaronga in 1942, pp. 102-103; loss of destroyer Teruzuki in December of 1942, pp. 106-107; treatm of survivors of U.S. ship sinkings in 1942, p. 109; presence on Savo Island, p. 112; successful elusion of torpedoes from Melhorn's planes of 24 July 1945, pp. 126-127; damage to battleship Haruna in July 1945, p. 127.

Lee, Rear Admiral Willis A., JR, USN (USNA, 1908)
As Commander Task Force 64 was expected to come in as reinforcement after 13 November 1942 Guadalcanal action, but because his arrival time was unpredictable and a Japanese

battleship task force was imminently due, Melhorn's PT squadron was sent out to engage the enemy, pp. 97-98.

Lend-Lease Program
Melhorn's nephew Franklin Lindsay's secretive role in U.S. aid to Russia from Teheran in the early 1940s, p. 63; Naval Medical Supply Depot in Brooklyn provides material to Russia, p. 65.

Lindsay, Franklin A.
Melhorn's nephew and future president and chairman of the board of Itek Corporation as an army officer during World War II, pp. 63-64; post-war positions as possible outcome of Melhorn's guidance to Lindsay while a student at Stanford, pp. 62, 64, 71.

Litvinoff, Maxim
As Russian delegate to World Disarmament Conference drew great interest when speaking on the Japanese bombing of Shanghai in 1932, pp. 48-49.

Madden, Lieutenant Commander George B., USN (USNA, 1931)
As commanding officer of the high speed transport Colhoun (APD-2) in 1942 and a stickler for decorum, decreed that his ship's officers wear service white uniforms, an order that was not always suitable for their tasks and that sometimes imperilled their lives, pp. 86-88.

Marine Corps Operations
Fourth Marine Regiment to Santo Domingo in 1915, pp. 10-14; in Haiti in 1915, p. 22; in Haiti in 1920, pp. 24, 26-28; detachment sent to Martinique in mid-1941 to neutralize French carrier posing threat to the Panama Canal, but they are recalled when a diplomatic solution is reached, pp. 81-82; First Marine Raider Battalion, under LCOL Edson, embarks on high speed transports to patrol the East Coast in 1941-1942, pp. 81-81; Second Marine Raider Battalion trains under LCOL Carlson near San Diego in 1942, pp. 82-85; First Marine Raider Battalion prepares in the Fiji Islands for Guadalcanal campaign in July of 1942, pp. 85-86.

McCain, Admiral John S., USN (USNA, 1906)
Melhorn's admiration of McCain as a task and carrier force commander during World War II from an aviator's standpoint, pp. 133-134.

McCawley, USS (AP-10)
With Rear Admiral Richmond Turner embarked as Commander Amphibious Force South Pacific in mid-1942 this transport took the ill Ensign Melhorn aboard after Guadalcanal action using a tank loading hook, pp. 90-91.

Medals
> See: Awards

Medicine
> Care for U.S. Marines in Santo Domingo in the mid-1910s, pp. 11-12; conditions at contagious disease camp at Norfolk in late 1910s, pp. 15-19; medical practice in Haiti in early 1920s, pp. 25-28; vaccination for smallpox epidemic in Haiti in 1920s, pp. 25-26; conditions in Haiti while Melhorn was chief of the Public Health Service in Haiti in the late 1920s, pp. 34-39.

Melhorn, Commander Charles M., USN
> Birth in Norfolk in 1918, p. 18; mix-up with trains as he visits parents in Europe after World Disarmament Conference in 1932 at age 13, p. 51; in 1932 enrages Swiss crowds at train station by giving Hitler salute, p. 52; education and path to commission in the Navy in 1941, pp. 78-80; family, pp. 78, 90, 96; "dry dock cruise" on USS New York (BB-34) 1940-1941, p. 79; duty on USS Gregory (APD-3) and USS Colhoun (APD-2) as part of a high speed transport squadron in early 1940s, pp. 80-91; as boat officer with APD squadron trains with U.S. Marines under LCOL Evans Carlson near San Diego in 1942, pp. 82-85; pneumonia prevents participation in Guadalcanal landings in August of 1942, but witnesses some shipboard action on Colhoun, pp. 86-90; removed from Colhoun for medical attention at mobile hospital in Auckland, pp. 90-91; part of the crew sent to retrieve the unmanned minesweeper USS Vireo (AM-52) in October, 1942, pp. 92-93; duty with Motor Torpedo Squadron Three in late 1942, pp. 93-102, 113-117; witness to fierce Guadalcanal assault on 12-14 November 1942, pp. 94-100; one of two survivors of a violent PT boat sinking off Tassafaronga in December of 1942, pp. 103-113; plane crash with instructor during flight training at Grand Prairie, Texas in 1943, pp. 117-120; operational duty with a torpedo plane squadron in Florida in the mid-1940s, pp. 120-125; midair collision on training bomb run off Miami, pp. 122-124; executive and commanding officer of torpedo squadron at Klamath Falls, Oregon in mid-1940s, p. 125; Melhorn's squadron deploys aboard USS Cowpens (CVL-25) in spring of 1945, pp. 125-132; reminiscences of fleet-long flyover at war's end in 1945, pp. 131-132; receives Navy Cross for damage inflicted on Japanese battleship Haruna in July 1945, p. 134; in commission crew of USS Leyte (CV-32) as flight deck officer in 1946, p. 134; flag secretary to Commander Carrier Division Four, 1949-1950, pp. 135-143; deploys with air group aboard USS Ticonderoga (CVA-14) in mid-1950s, pp. 143-150; loses plane during Mediterranean deployment in 1955, pp. 145-146; when Ticonderoga breaks mooring line while in port in Beirut, Melhorn is able to lessen damage to use of his planes in "pinwheel" formation in fall of 1955, pp. 146-150; duty on staff of Commander Carrier Division 15 in the late 1950s, p. 150; furthers education after retirement in 1961, pp. 151-153.

Melhorn, Rear Admiral Kent C., MC, USN
    Birth in 1883 and early years, pp. 1-3; family, pp. 3, 18, 30, 40, 43, 50-52, 74-75; commissioned into naval medical corps in 1907, pp. 1-3; duty on screw frigate Wabash in 1908, pp. 3-4; duty on screw steamer Yankee, including evacuation after it ran aground in 1908, pp. 4-6; duty on screw steamer Dixie, including attendance at inaugural parade for President Taft in 1909, pp. 6-7, 60; passed assistant surgeon at naval hospital at Newport, Rhode Island, 1911-1913, p. 7; duty aboard cruiser Denver (C-14) off coast of Nicaragua in mid-1910s, pp. 7-9; duty with Fourth Marine Regiment in San Diego in 1914, pp. 9-10; deployment as battalion surgeon with Marines to Santo Domingo in 1915 to help squelch revolution, pp. 10-14; received letter of commendation from Secretary of the Navy Josephus Daniels for performance of duty in Santo Domingo in the mid-1910s, p. 14; first lieutenant of naval corps at Norfolk Naval Hospital at outset of American involvement in World War I in charge of contagious disease camp, pp. 14-19; stationed in Haiti as commanding officer of general hospital from 1920 to 1923, pp. 19-31; plane crash in Haiti when returning from a medical emergency call, pp. 26-29; additional schooling at Massachusetts General Hospital under Dr. Paul White in 1923, pp. 29-30; embarrassed when mother-in-law contacts influential friend in the Senate to help his career in the mid-1920s, pp. 30-31; teaching duty at Naval Medical School in mid-1920s, pp. 31-33; endorsed by Rockefeller Foundation to be chief of Public Health Service in Haiti in the late 1920s, pp. 33-41, 43; kudos received for work in Haiti in the late 1920s, pp. 41-42, 73; detail officer at Bureau of Medicine and Surgery in 1930, pp. 45-53; goes to Geneva to attend to U.S. delegates at the World Disarmament Conference in 1932, pp. 45-53; fleet medical officer on the staff of commander in chief of the U.S. Fleet, 1935-1936, pp. 53-55; executive officer of the naval hospital at San Diego, and while on temporary duty as commanding officer has difficulty concerning dental care for an admiral's wife in the mid-1930s, pp. 55-58; duty in charge of dispensaries in Long Beach and San Pedro in the late 1930s, p. 57; fleet medical officer, Pacific Fleet, 1939-1941, pp. 60-63; duty in charge of Naval Medical Supply Depot, Brooklyn from 1941-1946, pp. 63-72; medals and citations awarded throughout career, pp. 72-74; retired life, 1946-1970, pp. 75-76; Charles M. Melhorn's father influences his decision to enter the Navy after graduating from college in 1940, p. 78; his friendship with Rear Admiral Richmond Turner helps expedite his son's removal from the high speed transport Colhoun (APD-2) for medical attention in 1942, p. 90.

Meredith, USS (DD-434)
    While accompanying the old minesweeper Vireo (AM-52) which was towing aviation fuel to Guadalcanal in October of 1942, a Japanese task force was sighted and the crew of Vireo was put aboard this ship for safety. Meredith was then sunk by Japanese aircraft with a heavy loss of life, p. 92.

Midway, USS (CVB-41)
    As flagship for commander of Carrier Division Four (RADM Joseph "Jocko" Clark) in 1950, this carrier was the site of a celebrity-studded party during which crew members had to use innovative methods to get incapacitated guests aboard, pp. 138-142.

Motor Torpedo Squadron Three
    Many personnel in squadron were survivors of the USS Hornet (CV-8) sinking in October of 1942, pp. 93-94; Melhorn and group of mechanics on way to Tulagi narrowly miss involvement in 13 November 1942 Guadalcanal action, p. 94; as only firepower left on Tulagi, sent out on an unsuccessful mission to encounter Japanese battleship task force on night of 13 November 1942, pp. 97-99; mistakenly fire on damaged USS Portland (CA-33) while in search of Japanese battleships, p. 99; interdiction patrols to protect Guadalcanal after victory, pp. 100-101; picks up survivors of cruisers damaged during Battle of Tassafaronga in late 1942, pp. 102-103; Melhorn is an observer on PT-44 when sunk in December of 1942, pp. 103-113; squadron stationed aboard gunboat USS Jamestown (PG-55) in December of 1942, pp. 113-115.

Naval Academy, U.S.
    Kent Melhorn's early desire to attend changed by his fear of flunking out, p. 3; first experience with alumni officers in 1908 on board USS Wabash is disillusioning, p. 4; Charles Melhorn attends three-month course for deck volunteer general (DVG) officers in 1941, p. 79; animosity of midshipmen toward DVG, both because of their quick path to a commission and the accommodations made for them, pp. 79-80; armed guard school conducted to prepare naval officers for duty on board merchant ships in transatlantic convoys in 1941, p. 80; hazing incident involving midshipmen Joseph Clark and Forrest Sherman around time of World War I, p. 135.

Naval Medical Corps
    Size in mid-1920s, p. 31.

Naval Medical Supply Depot; Brooklyn, New York
    Organization at the outset of U.S. entry into World War II, pp. 65, 69; Undersecretary of the Navy Forrestal sends management team to inspect organization which nets a talented staff officer for Melhorn, pp. 70-71; British naval pharmacist requested by Melhorn to coordinate supply procedure, p. 72.

Nicaragua
    Cruiser USS Denver (C-14) patrols west coast in the mid-1910s, p. 8; residents of Chinandega beat cocky Denver team in baseball in mid-1910s, pp. 7-9.

Norfolk Naval Base Hospital
    Condition of contagious disease camp in the late 1910s, pp. 15-17, 19; Melhorns' living quarters, p. 18.

Pearl Harbor, Hawaiian Islands
    Admiral Richardson as commander in chief of the Pacific Fleet in the late 1930s advocated movement of battleships throughout the Pacific versus massing at Pearl Harbor, and was promptly removed from his position, pp. 60-61; Japanese sub patrolled entrance to harbor in late 1930s, pp. 61-62; Melhorn's reaction upon hearing of Japanese attack in December of 1941 while stationed in Brooklyn, p. 68.

Pendleton, Colonel Joseph H., USMC (USNA, 1882)
    As commanding officer of Fourth Marine Regiment during deployment to Santo Domingo in mid-1910s displayed calmness during intense action which bolstered Melhorn's courage, pp. 10, 13-14.

Pennsylvania, USS (BB-38)
    Melhorn has duty as fleet medical officer aboard this battleship which served as flagship for the commander in chief of the U.S. Fleet in the mid-1930s, Admiral Joseph M. Reeves, pp. 53-55, 61-62.

Pinwheel maneuver
    Melhorn initiates the use of the AD-5W Skyraiders in his squadron aboard the USS Ticonderoga (CVA-14) to execute this maneuver to lessen damage when the carrier broke a mooring line near Beirut in 1955, pp. 147-150.

Portland, USS (CA-33)
    As Melhorn watched from Tulagi, this cruiser could only circle aimlessly after a Japanese torpedo damaged her rudder during Guadalcanal action on 13 November 1942, p. 96; a motor torpedo boat from Melhorn's squadron mistakenly fires four torpedoes at Portland while in search of Japanese battleships on the night of 13 November 1942, p. 99.

Prisoners of war
    Melhorn flew member of Admiral Halsey's staff to Atsugi, Japan in August of 1942 to arrange for exchanges with the Japanese, pp. 129-131.

PT Operations
    See: Motor Torpedo Squadron Three

Public Health Service, Haiti
    Medical facilities in 1920s, p. 25; health problems in early 1920s, pp. 25-26; Haitian anesthetist proves more capable than U.S. Marine doctor after Melhorn's plane crash in early 1920s, p. 28; advances made during Melhorn's tour as head of the Public Health Service in the late 1920s, pp. 34-37; effect of Haitian racism on medical appointments, pp. 38-39.

Raider Battalions, U.S. Marine Corps
See: Marine Corps Operations, United States

Reeves, Admiral Joseph M., USN (USNA, 1894)
Melhorn's admiring recollection of his public speaking talent as commander in chief of the U.S. Fleet in the mid-1930s, pp. 53-54.

Richardson, Admiral James O., USN (USNA, 1902)
As commander in chief of the Pacific Fleet in the late 1930s was abruptly removed by President Roosevelt after expressing the view that battleships should not be moored en masse at Pearl Harbor, pp. 60, 66; after retirement offers explanation to Melhorn of his feelings on 7 December 1941, pp. 65-66.

Rockefeller Foundation
Offered philanthropic grant to establish medical school in Haiti and endorsed Melhorn as chief of Public Health Service there in the late 1920s, pp. 34, 38.

Rosenblatt, Lieutenant Herman S., USNR
Political and celebrity connections that this flag secretary and New York lawyer passed along to his close associate and former boss, Admiral Joseph "Jocko" Clark, in the 1940s made the admiral none too popular with his peers, pp. 136-138, 142.

Sam, Milbrun Gjuillaume
Upon his murder in 1915 as president of Haiti, U.S. Marines entered the country to ensure that the Germans could not get an easier access to the Panama Canal, pp. 22-23.

Santo Domingo
See: Dominican Republic

Savo Island, Solomon Islands
Burial practices caused concern to Melhorn as he was feebly swimming to shore because they attracted sharks, p. 111; although there were Japanese on the island, the natives sided with the Allies and helped Melhorn's rescue effort in 1942, p. 112.

Searles, Lieutenant, junior grade John M., USNR
While in command of a motor torpedo boat in Melhorn's squadron sank a Japanese submarine in December of 1942 with the help of very precise intelligence provided by Pacific Fleet headquarters, pp. 100-101.

Sharks
Caused Melhorn concern as he swam from motor torpedo boat sinking towards Savo in December of 1942, pp. 111-113; attacked bodies from Melhorn's PT sinking, p. 113.

Sinkings
    See: Accidents/Disasters

Sixth Fleet operations
    Animosity between Vice Admiral Forrest Sherman and Rear
    Admiral Joseph Clark surfaces during Mediterranean cruise
    in 1949, p. 136; USS Midway (CVB-41) site of party hosted
    by RADM Clark in 1950, pp. 138-142; accident-ridden cruise
    of USS Ticonderoga (CVA-14) in 1955, pp. 143-150; lack
    of opportunity to practice instrument landings aboard
    Ticonderoga during 1955 cruise and subsequent difficulties,
    pp. 144-146; pinwheel maneuver employed with AD-5W Skyraiders
    aboard Ticonderoga near Beirut in 1955 when mooring line
    breaks, pp. 146-150.

Skidmore, Ensign Lemuel, USNR
    Future high-powered New York lawyer has an inglorious night
    after the USS Jamestown's Christmas party in 1942, p. 115.

Smallpox
    Severe epidemic spreads through Haiti in the early 1920s
    which Melhorn believes was caused by the presence of this
    disease in Jamaica and the British Government's refusal
    to acknowledge it in order to protect tourism, pp. 25-26.

Spratling, Captain Leckinski, MC, USN
    As commanding officer of the naval hospital in Norfolk
    requested coffin builders from the commandant of the Navy
    Yard to meet a flu epidemic in the late 1910s, p. 16.

Stassen, Captain Harold E., USNR
    As staff officer in Halsey's Third Fleet organization was
    flown by Melhorn to Atsugi, Japan, to arrange prisoner
    of war exchanges and demonstrated fearlessness with potentially
    hostile Japanese, pp. 129-131.

Swanson, Claude A.
    Melhorn goes to Geneva to attend this Democratic senator
    from Virginia while he is a delegate to the World Disarmament
    Conference in 1932, pp. 45-46.

Swimming--survival at sea
    Melhorn's eight hour ordeal in the Pacific after the
    destruction of PT-44 in December of 1942, pp. 108-113;
    after midair collision during operational training with
    a torpedo plane squadron in the mid-1940s Melhorn remains
    in the water for several hours until rescued by the Coast
    Guard, p. 124.

Taft, William Howard
    Melhorn attends the inaugural parade of the 27th President
    of the United States on 4 March 1909 while stationed on
    screw steamer Dixie, pp. 6-7.

Tanaka, Rear Admiral Raizo, IJN
   As extremely capable commander of a destroyer squadron wreaked havoc on American cruisers with very little effort at the Battle of Tassafaronga in November of 1942, pp. 102-103.

Teruzuki, HIJMS
   After this destroyer was damaged during Guadalcanal action at Tassafaronga in December of 1942 PT-44 with Melhorn aboard passed her, only to become an easy target when she went up in flames, pp. 106-107.

Ticonderoga, USS (CVA-14)
   Large number of accidents and fatalities during Mediterranean cruise in 1955, pp. 143-146; struck U.S. destroyer while in port near Beirut, Lebanon, when a mooring line broke in mid-1950s, pp. 146-150.

Training, Naval
   Shipboard duty and three months of land-based classes as path for commissioning for those in the V-7 program in early 1940s, pp. 78-80; armed guard school held at the U.S. Naval Academy in 1941 to prepare naval officers for transatlantic convoy duty aboard merchant vessels, p. 80; boat officers train with Marines in the San Diego area in mid-1942, pp. 83-85.

Ultra
   See: Intelligence

Tone, HIJMS
   Japanese heavy cruiser assigned as a target to Melhorn's squadron on 24 July 1945, but eluded their torpedoes, pp. 126-127.

Torpedo plane operations
   While with an operational training squadron in the mid-1940s Melhorn is involved in a midair collision, pp. 120-125; as commanding officer of a squadron deploys aboard USS Cowpens (CVL-25) in 1945, pp. 125-132; sinking of Japanese battleship Haruna by Melhorn's squadron on 28 July 1945, pp. 126-127; even after atomic bombs dropped in August of 1945 sent on raids in Japan, pp. 127-128; participation in ceremonial flyover and other tasks after Japanese surrender pp. 129-132.

Turner, Rear Admiral Richmond K.
   As commander, Amphibious Force South Pacific and a good friend of Melhorn's father, facilitates an ill ENS Melhorn's removal from Colhoun (APD-2) to get medical attention to August of 1942, pp. 90-91; assigns Melhorn to a motor torpedo (PT) squadron in November of 1942, p. 93.

Uniforms, naval
    Insistence of the commanding officer of the transport Colhoun
    (APD-2) that his officers wear service whites regardless
    of duty, even during the Guadalcanal landings in August
    of 1942, pp. 86-88.

V-7 Program
    Melhorn's experiences going through this three month path
    to commissioning in 1940, pp. 78-80.

Vireo, USS (AM-52)
    Upon sighting of a Japanese task force in October, 1942
    all hands were removed from this elderly minesweeper to
    the safety of the accompanying destroyer Meredith (DD-434),
    which was subsequently attacked and sunk; Melhorn was one
    of a crew later sent to retrieve the Vireo as she floated,
    unmanned, in the Pacific, pp. 92-93.

Wabash, USS (screw frigate)
    Melhorn's first duty station after graduating from the
    Naval Medical School in 1908 was aboard this receiving
    ship at the Boston Navy Yard, and it was while serving
    in Wabash that he had his first contact with a Naval Academy-
    graduated officer, pp. 3-4.

Webb, Rear Admiral Ulys R., MC, USN
    Caused Melhorn to be detached prematurely from the San
    Diego Naval Hospital in the mid-1930s after he refused
    to allow dental care privileges for Webb's wife, pp. 56-57.

Williams, First Lieutenant Ernest C. "Bill", USMC
    Melhorn assesses Williams as greatest soldier he has ever
    known and describes his heroic capture of a fort held by
    rebels in Santo Domingo in 1917, pp. 11-12; model for character
    in play "What Price Glory?," p. 12; assignments arranged
    by influential member of Congress, p. 13.

Woolley, Mary E., Ph.D.
    As U.S. delegate to the World Disarmament Conference in
    1932 was a vociferous pacifist who did not command much
    attention to her demand for unilateral disarmament, pp.
    47, 49-50.

World Disarmament Conference; Geneva, Switzerland 1932
    Melhorn's recollections of meetings attended while on temporary
    attachment to the General Board of the Navy, pp. 47-50.

World War II
    Guadalcanal campaign (August to November, 1942), pp. 86-100;
    Battle of Tassafaronga (November to December, 1942), pp.
    102-108; use of the atomic bomb in mid-1945, pp. 127-128;
    Japanese surrender in August of 1945, pp. 129-132.

Yankee, USS (screw steamer)
    Melhorn's experiences abandoning ship after the Yankee ran
    aground 23 September 1908 in Buzzards Bay, pp. 4-6.

www.ingramcontent.com/pod-product-compliance
Lightning Source LLC
Chambersburg PA
CBHW080612170426

43209CB00007B/1414